C000094871

Robert Schumann

Robert Schumann

HAUS PUBLISHING · LONDON

First published in Great Britain in 2004 by
Haus Publishing Limited
26 Cadogan Court, Draycott Avenue
London SW3 3BX

A CIP catalogue record for this book is available from the British Library

ISBN 1-904341-54-3

Designed and typeset in Garamond by
Palimpsest Book Production Limited, Polmont, Stirlingshire

Printed and bound by Graphicom in Vicenza, Italy

CONTENTS

Lieder
für die
Jugend
von
Robert Schumann.
Op. 79.

Formative Years

Nobody noticed the man in the flower-patterned dressing gown as he walked in the pouring rain across the Old Rhine Bridge in Düsseldorf. The crowds were all wearing fancy-dress, since it was Rose Monday – the culmination of the Carnival in Rhineland. The year was 1854. It was only when he jumped from the bridge into the river that some young trenchermen noticed him. They dragged the heavy man to the bank but had no idea where to take him, as he did not speak. Eventually someone recognised him as Robert Schumann, the music director, by now soaked to the skin and shivering with cold. He was escorted home in a noisy crowd of revellers. Schumann held his hands to his face, as if hiding behind the last of his masks – from childhood days he had sought refuge in disguises when he wrote and composed. Here in the city that had inspired his *Rhenish Symphony*, and where he had received a festive welcome just three and a half years earlier, Robert Schumann had finally acted in a way in which he had previously only dreamed of.

I dreamed that I drowned in the Rhine Schumann wrote in his diary (T1,51) in 1829. He had been keeping a diary since the beginning of 1827, trying to find an identity for himself. *I am not yet really certain what I am* (T1,30), and had been seeking answers from an early age. At fifteen he wrote a self-concious journal, and at Easter 1828 he put together excerpts from old diaries entitled *Quintessential Extracts from the Youthful Sins or the Opinions and Thoughts, Right and Wrong, of the Poor Student Jeremiah – attempts at self-analysis,* trying to answer the question: Is this you or is it not? (T1,75,23).

While his mother was ill with typhus Schumann had been separated from his family for two and a half years, and he felt then he was not *a child like other children* (Q10). Later, at the Lyceum, this feeling of difference grew when his fellow pupils admired the future writer in him. He expressed this feeling in the various names he invented for himself. It was evident also in his aspiration to be great in one way or another: to be a *superior being*. 'He was quite

August Schumann. Painting by Leberecht Gläser, 1810

certain he would be a famous man one day – in what way he was not yet sure, but famous come what may', a school friend remembered.[1] The idea that fame might confer identity might have come from the work he did in helping his father, August Schumann, to compile short biographical articles for *his Portraits of Famous People from all Nations and Periods* – at fourteen Robert wrote several articles for this series.

August Schumann, the son of an impoverished pastor, had painfully realised at an early age how his own interests – in his case a love of literature, writing and sciences – conflicted with the realities of life. He began a commercial apprenticeship at fourteen, continuing to read widely on his own, and eventually enrolled as a student in the faculty of humanities at Leipzig University, only to drop out again when his savings ran out. He wrote novels and did translations, amongst other things, before becoming a bookseller. In 1807 he and his brother founded a bookshop and publishing house in Zwickau as the 'Gebrüder

The marketplace in Zwickau. Watercolour by Bruno Priemer, 1813

Schumann'. When Robert Schumann was baptised, the church register described his father as 'esteemed citizen and book-seller'. This elevated social status was achieved during wartime and epidemics, in difficult conditions that took their toll on his health. He was constantly ill, dying of tuberculosis at the age of just fifty-three. He left 60,000 talers, a small fortune, to his wife and four sons, of which the youngest, Robert, still a minor, inherited 10,323 talers.

August Schumann had published the works of several authors in collected editions. He also founded a weekly journal, translated Walter Scott and Lord Byron and published the classics of international literature in an affordable pocket edition, thereby contributing to the general level of education. 'I never saw him do anything but work', wrote Emil Flechsig,[2] Robert Schumann's school friend. His house in the Amtsgasse (now the Burgstrasse), purchased in 1817, had a private library containing 'the classical treasures of the whole world'.[3] This quiet, introverted man was particularly attached to his youngest son. Every day after dinner he would listen to Robert playing the Streicher grand piano, specially acquired on his behalf, and he tried in vain to persuade the famous Carl Maria von Weber to take his son as a pupil. *I enjoyed the most caring and loving upbringing,*[4] Robert Schumann wrote. As an adult he read the diaries and letters of his *wonderful father* (T1,165), whom he placed alongside the elevated mortals, the nobler souls. His mother, on the other hand, was mostly responsible for everyday matters. Robert resembled his father in many ways: in the

Christiane Schumann. Painting by Leberecht Gläser

variety of his interests, in his application and his organisational skills, and in his determination to live with and for art.

Christiane Schumann regarded her youngest son, who was born on 8 June 1810, as her 'golden boy', someone special (Q 15). She was musical herself and made sure that at the age of seven he was sent to the Zwickau organist, Johann Gottfried Kuntsch, for piano lessons. Schumann seems to have seen his mother as a strict disciplinarian, who instilled in him a code of moral responsibility and the values of a bourgeois life: work hard, behave correctly, and prepare for a useful and respected career. His letters to her when a student often reveal a need to dissimulate, while his mother, particularly when she was depressed, often generated feelings of guilt in him. This is evident from his nightmares (Jb 174,232), his harsh words of self-reproach, and his constant resolutions for *moral improvement* (T1,24).

Robert Schumann's three older brothers all became booksellers and publishers. Their father died shortly after the suicide of their sister, Emilie, aged twenty-nine, who had been suffering from severe depression. After August Schumann's death the guardianship of the youngest member of the family was assumed by Gottlob Rudel, a cloth and iron merchant in Zwickau, who was conscientious in his attention to financial matters. Robert Schumann learned Latin from the age of seven at the excellent private school run by Dr Döhner in Zwickau, with Greek and French the following year. He moved to the Lyceum at Easter 1820, where he showed a marked talent for languages. He had many interests – these changed regularly, but were always passionate. It might be a *passion for the theatre*; or he would be gripped by the enigmatic genius of Hölderlin, Byron or Beethoven, then he fell into *an obsessive yearning for mu*sic (Q18). This unrest was evident in the swift mood swings of the following years. Meanwhile he proved in practical ways that he was no mere passionate dreamer. In 1825 he set up a youth orchestra and a literary club, devised programmes for 'evening recitals and discussions' (Q20), and was assiduous in all the arrangements for these.

Robert Schumann's musical education up to 1828 remained that of an amateur, and seems provincial alongside that of his almost exact contemporary Felix Mendelssohn. Comparing the training Mendelssohn received, so very different from his own – an outstanding teacher, Carl Friedrich Zelter, the opportunity to meet famous artists and scientists in his parents' Berlin home, nine string symphonies composed by the age of fifteen, followed just two years later by the *Midsummer Night's Dream* overture, a work of international significance – Schumann felt he was at a bitter disadvantage: *If I had grown up in similar circumstances, destined from childhood for a musical career, I would absolutely soar above you all – the power of my imagination makes me feel this,* he wrote to Clara Wieck in 1838 (Jb283f). Schumann's knowledge of music was acquired at the 'Bürger Konzerte' in Zwickau, where the performers were amateurs or military musicians; operas were usually presented in piano reduction, Beethoven's symphonies as piano duets. Quartets were performed at private soirées in the homes of Schlegel, the postmaster, and Carus, a manufacturer. Schumann himself played the piano at many a 'musical evening' and school concert. His piano teacher, who *was himself only an average performer* (Q12) soon advised that his pupil should teach himself from now on. So Schumann's playing consisted primarily of *improvising,* and his comical piano portraits of his friends, with apt likenesses that made his audience laugh, demonstrate not only his talents at improvisation but also his good critical eye.

When he was twelve Schumann played the piano part for a performance of Friedrich Schneider's *Last Judgement* in the Marienkirche at Zwickau. This made such an impression on him that he composed a setting of Psalm 150 for voice, piano and orchestra, Op 1, despite never having had a single lesson in harmony or counterpoint.

He also wrote several numbers for an opera. It was in the Carus home in Zwickau that he met Agnes Carus, the wife of a doctor from Colditz who was

Title page of Psalm 150. The eleven-year-old already saw himself as an artist and added the address of the famous German publisher 'chez Breitkopf et Härtel' to his name shortly to become professor of medicine at the university in Leipzig. This was in the summer of 1827. It was through her that he discovered the music of Schubert. He was permitted to accompany her on the piano as she sang Schubert Lieder, and she also encouraged him to write his own songs, Op 2. Schumann's diaries for the following two years are a clear indication of his youthful admiration for Agnes Carus. His thoughts of her *saintly image*, are evident in his piano fantasias and in his dreams at this time (T1,86). His letters and diary entries, written in a melancholy and sentimental style, about his meetings with Liddy Hempel and Nanni Petsch, on whom he had a schoolboy crush, make clear the dichotomy in the young Schumann's feelings about women: he longed for a love *found in divine contemplation and worship* (W27), a sort of *Madonna worship* (Jb5), revealed in symbols, as described in his *Juniusabende*, while he was disgusted by his own desires, his *commonness and vulgarity* (Jb10).

In his parents' house there was much more literature than there was music, so Schumann's interests during his schooldays were predominantly literary. He translated Latin and Greek texts, and by 1826 was already offering his poems to the Dresden *Abend-Zeitung* (T1,439). He was trying the role of author, with pseudonyms such as *Fust, Robert an der Mulde, Skülander*, and *Robert Alantus*; he was contemplating dedications and drawing up a *project book*. Half in jest and half seriously he

Robert Schumann. Colour miniature, c. 1826

remarked in a letter to Flechsig in March 1828, *Our letters will be published one day, for sure* (Jb15). He experimented with various dramatic genres, but produced a mere handful of scenes. In December 1825 he had founded a literary society with ten fellow students at his school. In their 30 meetings up to February 1828 they read eight plays by Schiller, among other things, often each taking a part – their club statutes set out fines imposed for *unseemly* laughter.

It was clear to Schumann from his schooldays that his was a solitary nature, and this despite his leading role in the literary society and the youth orchestra, the Romantic friendship within the *Four-leaved Clover* (Schumann, Röller, Flechsig and Walther) and his *Klopstock evening walks* with his friends (T1,29; Jb17). Early in 1827 he was conducting dialogues with his diary, his *most trusted companion* (T1,417) instead of talking with other people. Sometimes these entries take the viewpoint of the imaginary reader – strange dedications, titles such as Jean Paul would have used, or aphorisms in the style of Novalis or Friedrich Schlegel. Even then Schumann was thought to be melancholy (T1,83). One reason for this growing introversion may have been the traumatic effect of his early encounters with mental illness and death. *The fair and fickle youth often smiles at me with his beautiful big eyes*, he wrote in May 1828 (T1,89). This feeling of *vulnerability* later became an obsession. The death of his father in August 1826 and the suicide of his sister the previous year had given him a manic fear of being abandoned. He dreamed of drowning 25 years before he actually jumped into the Rhine, because he wanted to die. When his sister-in-law Rosalie died in 1833, Schumann spent a *terrible night* and had dreadful panic attacks (W110); his brother's illness caused *continual dreams of home and Julius* (T1,216), and when news came of his death the attacks returned. He felt as if he was *a statue who could feel neither warmth nor cold*, and he was seized with *inexpressible fear*; he was afraid that *something might happen to him*, so he arranged for a fellow student to live with him. Again, when his close friend Ludwig Schuncke was dying in 1834, Schumann fled to Zwickau, and moved to new lodgings after his death.

The world lies before me . . . Now my true inner self must emerge and show himself, Schumann wrote after he had passed his final school examinations, his *Abitur*, with the second highest grade, 'omnino dignus' (Jb 13). The first thing he did was to make a pilgrimage to southern Germany with his friend Gisbert Rosen (W26). He wrote his impressions of this holiday in his diary: his tears at the grave of Jean Paul, his visit to *Heine's springtime house*, the poet's garden room in Munich and his *uplifting conversation* (T1,64) with the author he so admired (Heine's *Book of Songs* had been published the previous year), and finally his visit to Jean Paul's widow in Bayreuth. He wrote to his friend Rosen *If only the whole world could read Jean Paul, then it would certainly be a better place, if a less happy one – he often brought me close to madness* (NF5).

Robert Schumann was destined for the law – a decision made by his guardian Rudel, his mother and his brother Edward. His own unexpressed wish for an artistic life, rather than a useful career, could hardly compete with sound bourgeois principles, where the 'point' of human existence, as described ironically in E T A Hoffmann's *Kreisleriana*, consisted in becoming 'an efficient cogwheel in the mill of society'.[5] So, Robert Schumann went along with his family's decision and on 29 March 1828 he enrolled as a law student at the university in Leipzig. But his *constant inner conflict with this choice* of study dates from this point. He found *cold jurisprudence* repellent (Jb22), and his resentment is clear in a letter he wrote ten years later to Clara Wieck: *My father . . . meant me to become a musician, but my mother would not allow it* (Jb284).

Leipzig was the second largest city in Saxony, after Dresden, and had a population of 41,000. To Schumann it seemed *a huge great city* (Jb22) with its trade fairs, its bookshops and presses, its old and famous university, and with such well-known publishing houses as Breitkopf & Härtel, Brockhaus and Reclam. *The wonderful great concerts* in the Gewandhaus made him *blissfully happy* (NF13). Yet he was still homesick. When he rememb-

The Leipzig Gewandhaus. Anonymous engraving, c. 1830

ered *quiet autumn evenings at home* (Jb40) he often felt *thoroughly crushed and miserable* (NF11), *quite downcast* in this *horrible Leipzig* (Jb32,30). Although he repeatedly tried to reassure his mother that he was *regularly attending lectures* (Jb25), although he promised his guardian to work hard, *however icy cold and dry it might be to begin with* (NF6), he spent most of his time on music, writing and reading. Many a morning disappeared in *lyrical lounging* in his dressing gown, in *free improvisation* at the piano, followed by *Jean Pauliades* over coffee and cigars (T1,113). He played chess and whist, frequented the billiard room at the Kaffeebaum Restaurant, and occasionally took fencing lessons, in his opinion indispensable for cutting a *proper figure* (Jb25). From time to time he attended philosophy lectures, but he assured one friend that he had *not yet attended a single seminar* in his own faculty (NF9). Flechsig reports that Schumann never even set foot in a lecture hall.[6] There were frequent altercations with his fellow lodger, Emil Flechsig, whom the more sensitive Schumann often regarded as *a boor, devoid of spirit or any Promethean spark*, and most intolerable to Schumann was his piano-bashing (T1,107,115, 114).

Schumann joined a fraternity along with Moritz Semmel, a future lawyer and his brother-in-law, with whom he shared an interest in *philosophy, the republic,* and, *democracy* (T1,90) but his membership faded quickly. Carl Ernst Richter, editor of the satirical political magazine *Die Biene*, and an enthusi-

Emil Flechsig. Coloured drawing by A. Bach.

astic admirer of the French Revolution, had been one of Robert Schumann's most influential teachers at the Lyceum. In 1825 Schumann had founded a 'secret school society' (Q26) along revolutionary lines – quite a dangerous move considering the state's persecution of all liberation movements. But, as he lamented in 1829, *I had thought so highly of fraternity members, and how lacking I found most of them to be* (NF5). *The ideal of fraternity should be the moral, intellectual and physical education of the man, creating a public figure, a rounded whole,* Schumann wrote to his friend Rascher. *If this is what the students want, then they should not just sit in pubs and watch life pass them by, as they seem to do . . . That is no way to set the world to rights* (Q26). He was unhappy with the *affected Germanism* (T1,121) of the clubs and scoffed at *their airy-fairy, hazy concepts of national character* (NF5). Schumann and Semmel then joined the Marcomann Society to have some fun, so the diary that typically uses words such as *Hottentottiana* for the fencing hall, and references to occasional periods of *swotting,* to sybarism (NF4) with its *ups and its downs* (T1,130), to his taste for champagne, claret and beer, to morning *hangovers* and frequent *financial concerns* (T1, 144), necessitating applications for funds to his guardian or to his brother Eduard.

Schumann found that his *imagination was enhanced and soared* after alcohol, cigars and coffee (T1,97), and he depended on these stimulants when inspiration failed and he achieved nothing for months on end. The *snail's pace*[7] of the Leipzig years often induced *apathy and melancholy* (T1,118). In the diary of the time he describes his own *eternal Gordian knot: he thrashes and thrashes but cannot untie it, becoming ever more entangled* (T1,97 f). Uncertain of his own abilities, feeling that he lacks a core (T1,141), Schumann notes, *I feel an icy shiver down my spine as I wonder what is to become of me* (T1,84). He repeatedly summons his will-power: *I may and must not be weak* (Jb41).

If a man but has the will, he can do anything (Jb23). He read widely: Schelling, Fichte and Kant, Lessing, Hamann, Herder, Grabbe, Calderón and Byron were his bedtime reading. In the summer of 1828 Schumann wrote various prose pieces inspired by the overwhelming influence of Jean Paul. First *Juniusabende und July-tage*[8] (June Evenings and July Days), descriptions of nature as reflections of the mind,

Robert Schumann. Miniature on ivory, 1830

written from the perspective of a sensitive narrator on a romantic subject: the gulf between bleak reality and an Arcadian world seen in Nazarene colours, modelled on *Lilienbad*, the utopia of love, in Jean Paul's *Die unsichtbare Loge* (The Invisible Box). The parallels with his own life – improvisation at the piano, the loss of his sister, the death of his father – make it clear that this is autobiographical. The wish to write of himself (as Jean Paul did), as a different but real person, can be seen in the fragments of the humorous rite-of-passage novel, *Selene* (T1,150), which was to present the life of a *noble* man. *Gustav must pass through all the schools of life*, before he *finally* embodies that harmony of strength and gentleness (T1,139) that Schumann sought for himself. This can be seen from a note in the margin of the manuscript: *Speaking of myself now*. His protagonist, like his namesake in Jean Paul's novel *Die unsichtbare Loge*, reflects Schumann's own problems as he embarked on his studies, *feeling cast adrift into life, flung headlong into the darkness of the world* (Jb13). Two other figures were also to feature in his novel, the admirable Prince Louis Ferdinand of Prussia, whose music Schumann often listened to and played at this time, and Jean Paul whom he venerated *above all others* (Jb17) – signs here of Schumann's attempt to break down the boundary between fiction and reality. The graveyard serves as a metaphor for the world in which Gustav grows up, while in Schumann's first literary work, *Juniusabende und Julytage,* the world is seen as symbolic of *a monstrous graveyard for defunct dreams*. Here we can see how Schumann and his contemporaries felt themselves to be merely the 'shadows' and 'echoes'[9] of their predecessors. In the absurd scenes of *Selene*, the reader cannot be certain whether the figures are meant to be spectres, as allegory or are completely alienated.[10] They are early examples of the 'curse' of the early nineteenth century, that Karl Immermann described in his novel *Die Epigonen*: 'feeling ill-fated yet with no especial grief'.[11]

Schumann's quest for an individual identity is evident again in the *Fantasie Scherzante Ueber Genial- Knill- Original- und andre itäten*.[12] He believed that feeling and reason were reconciled in the man of genius. Schumann had also studied the writings of Christian Daniel Schubart and Jean Paul on the aesthetics of music, as can be seen in *Die Tonwelt*,[13] a short work written jointly with his friend Willibald von der Lühe, in which music is celebrated as *an earthly glimpse of the beyond*, as the language above all other languages, comprehensible only to the *higher* man. The epigraph of this work shows how close it was to Jean Paul's *Hesperus*. It ends with a homage to Beethoven, and makes clear Schumann's passionate dislike at this period of all the *theory of the physical and intellectual nourishment in music*. He was, however, capable of seeing some irony in his own *Jean Pauliaden. We do not seem to have thoroughly digested Jean Paul,* he remarked in March 1828 (Jb15); and when he read over his old works three years later he noted: *Good Heavens! how wrong these feelings are! and how much I had to laugh!* (T1,372).

Schumann was living on the first floor at 454 Auf dem Brühl, 'exceptionally elegant student lodgings' that were 'particularly well suited for music-making'.[14] There were trio and quartet evenings, with Täglichsbeck playing the violin, Sörgel the viola, Glock the cello, and with Schumann, who smoked the most cigars, at the piano. They played Schubert's Trio in E flat major, D929 (T1,152), as well as his *Lieder*,[15] the *Wanderer Fantasia*, some of his waltzes, the polonaises and Variations For Four Hands, D908, *the most perfect romantic portrait, a whole novel in music* (T1,96), that Schumann *'loved madly'*,[16] and that would inspire him to compose his own duets – Eight Polonaises and Variations on a theme by Prince Louis Ferdinand of Prussia. When he learned of Schubert's death, in November 1828, a neighbour heard Schumann 'sobbing the whole night through'.[17]

Schumann was invited to the house of Professor Carus, a great art lover, and he went each time with heart pounding in the expectation of seeing Agnes Carus. Here he made the acquaintance of Heinrich Marschner, the musical director of the Leipzig Theatre, whose opera *Der Vampyr* had been his breakthrough at its premiere in March. Several numbers from the opera were to be performed. He also met Gottfried Wilhelm Fink, the editor of the Leipzig *Allgemeine Musikalische Zeitung*, Julius Knorr, a pianist who later became a colleague on Schumann's periodical, as well as the conductor and composer Gottlob Wiedebein, who encouraged Schumann to compose. In July Schumann sent him his own settings of poems by Justinus Kerner for his *kind but critical opinion* (NF6), and Wiedebein's cordial reply made him *completely happy* (T1,102). It was, however, the meeting with Friedrich Wieck at the Carus's house that had the greatest consequences.

Friedrich Wieck was forty three years old at the time, and had recently married the young Clementine Fechner, his second wife. He had three children, Clara, Alwin and Gustav, from his first marriage to Marianne Tromlitz, from whom he was divorced in 1825. After completing his studies in theology, Wieck had worked as a tutor, before coming to social prominence. Later he

Friedrich Wieck teaching his daughter Clara. Plaster relief

established the first pianoforte business in Leipzig, ran a music lending library and was the first to introduce grand pianos made in the Viennese manner. He was a famous piano teacher, although he himself had had no formal musical training. As a progressive teacher he used a chiroplast, following the method of Bernhard Logier which was widespread at the time, and, like Logier, combined instruction at the keyboard with a thorough training in music theory.

His daughter Clara was a shining example of his method, especially after her debut at the Gewandhaus, on 20 October 1828, at the age of nine. Wieck also wrote on musical subjects and was a journalist, contributing articles to the *Leipziger Tageblatt* and later to the *Neue Zeitschrift für Musik*. Schumann was keen to submit himself to Wieck's strict teaching methods. He was fascinated by this *fiery man* (T1,110), who was soon to become his fatherly mentor. Wieck was interested in the 'somewhat moody, pig-headed but noble' young man,[18] but it became quite clear to Robert Schumann that in spite of his skill as a pianist he lacked elementary technical requirements. Schumann confessed as late as 1831 that *he could play all concerts from the music but fundamentally he would have to start with the scale of C major*

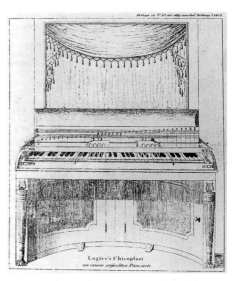

During his studies with Friedrich Wieck Schumann had to practise on a chiroplast, designed by Johann Bernhard Logiers. It was a study aid, which was supposed to correct the positioning of the hands by showing which key corresponded to which note on the scale above

(NF31). He practised his scales, half the time obediently, half in protest, and felt like a *musical novice in this scale-playing existence* (T1,128,149). At times he practised unwisely with the consequence that in December he was complaining of pains in his arm, and relapsed once more into *lyrical lounging*. Schumann often 'excused himself for 8 to 14 days, or even longer', according to Wieck (Q64), so this somewhat irregular tuition only lasted from August 1828 to February of the following year.

The next step was to be *the study of composition*, Schumann wrote to Wiedebein, since he had to admit that he was *ignorant of harmony, basso continuo and counterpoint* (NF7). Flechsig recalled the 'foolish position' in which Schumann composed: 'He was always puffing away on a cigar, pursing up his mouth and the glowing stub as far as he could and squinting down with his eyes, so the smoke made his eyes water and he pulled the most extraordinary faces'[19] – he was whistling tunes at the same time. His compositions in 1828 were not written for a virtuoso career: polonaises and variations for piano duet, songs, and the Piano Quartet in C minor. Schumann must now have felt himself considerably handicapped from never having learned harmony and counterpoint, since he soon began to find his own polonaises sounded wooden (T1,112,125); his songs, too, are not at all the *real portrayal* of his *inner self*, just imitations of his predecessors.[20] The Piano Quartet in C minor, however, on which he embarked at the end of November, shows a personal style. He noted a *feeling of great elation* when he had completed it, on 21 March 1829, after four months of hard work (T1,182). The opening movement, a sonata movement full of pathos in the style of Beethoven, clearly demonstrates the discrepancy between monumental style and technical deficiencies. On the other hand, in 1846 Schumann still recalled the *romantic trio*, and the originality of its fluid tonalities of C major and E minor, that embodied *a spirit turning its back on old music: a new poetic life* (T2,402). This is repeated, with slight changes, in the two following movements. The slow third movement explores the possibilities of polyphonic writing and uses strangely singing counterpoints in a way he would develop in later works. In the final movement Schumann made daring use of an ostinato rhythm almost all the way through, rather as Schubert did in several of his songs (*Erlkönig, Gretchen am Spinnrad*). The use of similar melodic material and repeated motifs and themes to unite the movements, and the economy of thematic material creating a wealth of melodies, are remarkable in such an early work. Soon, however, Schumann, with *a feeling of helplessness* (T1,223), must have felt dissatisfied with the harshness in the sound, and perhaps he also felt that his technical ability could not match his aspirations, since he planned a revision that he never carried out.

In early August 1828 Schumann had written in his diary: *Show them who you are* (T1,185), in an attempt to escape the *dreadful old rut* (Jb27) he had sunk into in Leipzig. As he explained to his mother, he wanted to *go to Heidelberg* for two semesters *to hear lectures by the most famous German lawyers, such as Thibaut and Mittermayer* (Jb30). In Heidelberg – the focal point for the previous generation of Romantic writers,

Page from the Piano Quartet c-minor

Brentano, Arnim, Eichendorff, Görres and the brothers Grimm – *where he so longed to be*, he would feel like a *son of the muses* (Jb60,54). He thought life in this city would be *pleasant and happy, not so grand, citified and varied as it was in Leipzig*. He would feel at home in Heidelberg, especially in the company of Rosen, whom he *regarded as a brother* (Jb62,107). The whole area, with its gentle, *lyrical ambience, like Provence* (Jb64), seemed idyllic to him, and what is more, Baden-Baden, Worms, Speyer and Mannheim were all within striking distance. He was soon *ensconced in a warm little study*, painted green like the one in Zwickau, and was firmly convinced that he had found his own *little home* (Jb87). But Schumann soon discovered there were disadvantages to a purely student-oriented town, where everything was *dearer, finer and nobler* (NF24). He spent *almost every evening in company or at balls,* there were plenty of young ladies *to court*, and he was *making his mark* with his *"galoppade"*. Life was expensive: restaurants only served set meals, and, apart from the expenses of his studies, he had to pay for *masked balls, tips, season tickets to the museums, cigars and more cigars – the piano tuner, the laundress, the bootboy, lights, soap*, and then there was champagne, music manuscript paper, books, *bills from his tailor and his cobbler*, rent for the piano and lessons in French, Italian, English and Spanish (JB104,65,70, 63,109,108). By the following year this *life of luxury* seemed a waste of time: *hours, nights and days we spent together, drinking, dreaming and gambling,* he wrote to a friend (BN31). Although Schumann had an annual income of 360 talers from interest on his capital,[21] he was soon in debt to the tune of 100 talers, and had to appeal to his guardian and to his brothers once again for assistance.

Justus Thibaut made the most lasting impression on Schumann during his time in Heidelberg. This famous lawyer had made his name with his legal book, *System des Pandektenrechts* (System of the Law of Pandects). He also directed the Heidelberg Choral

Society, and his book *Über Reinheit der Tonkunst* (Purity in Music) was published in 1824. As both a lawyer and a musician he demanded going 'back to the sources'. He conducted the Choral Society in Handel oratorios and a capella music from the Renaissance with an artistic sanctimoniousness that transfigured musical traditions to an idealised classical art form. Schumann took part in performances of works by Palestrina and Handel at Thibaut's house. *Thibaut is a wonderful, devout man . . . ; I am often unable to understand how a wretch like myself should have the honour of being admitted to listen in such a sacred house*, he wrote to his mother in February 1830 (Jb105). But Schumann, and others, were critical of Thibaut's rigid stance on early music, *his narrow-minded and truly pedantic view of music* (Jb81). Schumann's own piano quartet also showed his reaction against old music (T2,402). So he was of the opinion that: *Thibaut should be under the table with his Handel's opera arias* (Jb85).[22]

Travelling was, of course, vital for any student at Heidelberg. *There has been a buzzing in my heart since my earliest childhood, saying*

Evenings in the home of Professor Thibaut

'Italy, Italy', he wrote to his mother (Jb70) in a long letter with a plethora of arguments persuading her to finance this longed-for journey to Italy. On the Isola Bella he felt like Albanos, from Jean Paul's *Titan,* and for a few moments art and life were one. It was not visual art that fascinated him, but *the whole teeming activity of life itself* (NF19). He was entranced by the *forests of vines*, by the *gleaming white cities, by the perfumes of oranges and the flowers of the south,* by the sunsets and starry nights; most impressive of all were the *Junoesque Italian girls* (T1,267, 255, 258) *with their enormous, yearning, beautiful, fiery eyes* (NF19). Schumann wrote critically of Italian music, of its *sloppiness* and the *ardour with which they fiddle away all the time* (Jb81), but he was equally critical of the Italians' ignorance of literature (NF21). Although he was not a great admirer of Rossini, he preserved fond memories of Pasta and Lalande singing his arias in La Scala in Milan.

Poor as a beggar but filled with treasured memories, Schumann returned home on 20 October (Jb90,81). All his socialising in the summer of 1829 meant that his music studies had been relegated *very low* (Jb64), but in the winter they resumed more intensively than ever. His fellow student Röller might find him 'first thing in the morning sitting at the piano in his night-shirt practising Hummel exercises' (Q69). The *one and only Schubert* was still the central focus of his music studies (Jb82). Without doubt Schumann missed the Gewandhaus concerts and envied people in Leipzig the four Paganini concerts held there in October, but he himself had more opportunity for public performance in Heidelberg than in a large city like Leipzig. In January 1830 he performed the *Alexander Variations*, Op 32, by Moscheles in the 'Museum', a student music society of which he was a member. He had played these during the Easter vacation of 1829 in the Zwickau Music Society, and received *a good review in the little Zwickauer Wochenblätel* (T1,193). This time the calls of *'Bravo' and 'Encore'* . . . *went on and on, even the Grand Duchess applauded hard, and Schumann was soon the darling of Heidelberg audiences* (Jb104). The concert in the 'Museum' marked the end of his short career as a pianist – he never played in public again.

Schumann was not making as much progress as he had hoped in his own studies. Aggressively he decided to speed up his training by violent means. His thoughtless experiments with mechanical contraptions to restrict the movement of some fingers, thus strengthening others and helping them to work better individually, resulted in such pain that he could no longer even contemplate playing *finger exercises and scales* (BN28). It was only in the summer of 1830, when he had recovered to some extent, that he was able to resume practising three or four hours a day. He was developing a new self-awareness alongside the role of budding pianist, as he now regarded himself. He introduced himself as 'a sort of piano-player' (Q54), and wrote down and collected the comments of others on his piano playing. On 11 April 1830 he heard Niccolò Paganini play in Frankfurt, making the *driest exercises glow with Pythian ecstasy* (JD220). This experience *drove him to greater endeavour* (Q77) and fuelled his ambition. At the same time he maintained a critical distance, annoyed that the celebrated artist lacked the *grand and noble artistic composure of the priest* (T1,282).

But if you could only understand how my head is bursting with ideas, and how I would have reached my Op 100 if

Niccolò Paganini. Drawing by Johann Peter Lyser

only I could write down all my symphonies, he confided to Wieck. *I am sometimes so imbued with music, overflowing with notes that it is impossible for me to write anything down* (Jb83f). He did nevertheless manage to commit something to paper, as can be seen from the sketches for the *Abegg Variations*, Op 1, *Papillons* (Butterflies), Op 2, and the *Toccata,* Op 7, as well as his work on a Piano Concerto in F minor, and on the *Fandango*, later to influence the Sonata in F sharp minor. Apparently he was contemplating a musical career in November 1829, bolstered by Thibaut's remarks that *Heaven had not destined him to be a civil servant* (Jb115), when he told his mother *were I able to achieve anything in this world, it would be in music* (Jb92). His mother reacted with annoyance and depression, so he tried to reassure her that his concerts had been successful, and explained that the social status of a musician could be high, that he already had contacts amongst academics, privy councillors – even royalty itself. At the end of February 1830 Schumann asked that he be allowed to stay another semester in Heidelberg. He knew what *deathly monotony* awaited him as a lawyer: *an everlasting and deadly rut of wrangling and twopenny cases . . . everlasting subordination, nothing but legal papers and farmers, even if successful, a case of manslaughter* (Jb121,122). Entries in his diary in the spring of that year express his self-contempt and his doubts: *mutilating the piano . . . end of a miserable week . . . Alas! alas! . . . Terrible existence . . . Longing to throw myself into the Rhine* (T1, 227, 235, 236).

On 30 July 1830 Schumann informed his mother in the *most important* letter he *had ever written, or would ever write* (Jb119) that he had made the decision to become a musician. His whole life had been *a twenty-year-long conflict between poetry and prose*; now he was standing *at a crossroads. If I follow my genius,* he wrote, *I am led to art, which I believe to be the right way. But . . . it always seemed to me that you were really supporting me in this.* His ambition was a career as a virtuoso. Within six years he intended to *hold his own against any piano player* (Jb117,118). His next step would be tuition with Wieck, later perhaps with Moscheles in Vienna. He proposed that his mother should ask Wieck for his opinion. This was a first *step* from which his *whole future life*, his *fame* and his *happiness* would stem, and his relief at having at last made a decision was reflected in his renewed enthusiasm for work: he wanted to *shut himself away for three years* and to *hatch himself out* (Jb120,124). 'In fear and trembling', Christiane Schumann wrote to Wieck in a letter she found 'more difficult' than any she had ever written. She was 'worried about Robert's future', as he seemed to live in 'a higher sphere'; he should have embarked on a career as a pianist ten years earlier in order to earn 'his daily bread'; now he had 'studied for almost three years . . . and wasted a great deal' (W66,67). Wieck replied just two days later. He was convinced that he could make Robert Schumann, 'given his talent and his imagination, into one of the greatest living pianists within three years, who would play with more understanding and warmth than Moscheles, and better than Hummel'. But he set strict conditions: Schumann must curb his 'unreined imagination, and his widely swinging moods' and must study an hour a day for a year with himself in order to acquire the necessary 'lasting victory over the mechanics' (L1,21,22). Two years tuition in theory would also be required. Wieck wrote quite candidly of his doubts, and of the unreliability of his pupil, and recommended a trial period of six months. On this recommendation and on the advice of Professor Carus, Christiane Schumann allowed her son to decide for himself on his further course of study, although his brothers were not enthusiastic about a musical career. Now that the pressure of a mundane course of study was removed, Schumann felt enormously relieved. In the summer of 1830 he watched the movements for political liberation that followed the July Revolution with sympathy, and wrote a translation of the 'French Lord's Prayer' into his diary: *Our onetime King, who art a scoundrel, thy name be cursed, . . . , give us back this day the 46 millions, that you owe us* (T1,323). When an honorary doctorate was to be conferred on Schumann in 1840, he included in his biography his studies in philosophy and music at Leipzig and Heidelberg. He did not devote a single word to his studies in law.

The League of David

Schumann later wrote that his *real life* began after he had made his decision in favour of music, *that is, in the year 1830* (Bw95). Following the disastrous performance of his piano quartet at the end of January, he concentrated on a career as a pianist. He weighed up plans for various piano concertos; but his first published work should be a set of virtuoso concert variations with orchestra, like the *Don Giovanni Variations* by Chopin. Then he chose as his rather enigmatic theme something rather different from the fashion for brilliant variations on tunes from the operas of Rossini, Meyerbeer, Bellini, Donizetti or even from Mozart's *Don Giovanni*. He chose the name Abegg[23] (the letters of the name could be transformed as notes), and he dedicated the work to a certain Pauline, Comtesse d'Abegg. In order to be successful in the face of intense competition, concerto composers of his generation felt they had to be original at any price. The Comtesse was invented, but attention to this debut work was assured. Although in many of its virtuoso passages it showed the influence of contemporary bravura variations, in its final heavily reduced form, without orchestra, this was no virtuoso piece for the large concert hall. The theme, a sequence of broken chords, is in actual fact only a group of intervals and harmonic progressions. When the first five notes recur, they are concealed in middle parts or, in the finale, become a sort of negative as the sound gradually fades away. New figures are created from the first thematic interval, and at the conclusion of the third variation, when the metre breaks up, the way Schumann plays with the notes ABEGG in vertical and horizontal combinations is reminiscent of Bach, and not unlike modern permutation. New compositional methods and styles – harmonic expansion, syncopated shifted patterns, a progressive kind of tonality – give the music a dreamlike character. Critics were kind to Schumann's first opus, even Rellstab, *the most biting and the most feared*; novel aspects – the 'far-fetched' and the 'bizarre' – could be overlooked, and it was considered on the whole to be a 'wonderful bravura piece' (Jb171).

In October 1830 Schumann had moved into two rooms in Wieck's house, where his teacher not only lived, but also had his instrument store, a lending library and a pension for his students. It was here that he met Clara Wieck once again – now eleven years old. He had admired her piano playing two years earlier at Carus' house. Her musical education was following a strict programme: in addition to her piano lessons, she went to Heinrich Dorn for composition and instrumentation, while violin and singing lessons were added later. Her father regularly took her to the theatre and the opera, and to performances in private houses. A daily walk lasting several hours completed her schedule. Marianne Wieck had left her husband in May 1824, when Clara was four years old. For several months Clara was permitted to stay with her mother, but thereafter Wieck insisted on his rights to the three oldest children, so Clara grew up in her father's house with a series of housekeepers to look after her. At first she was thought to be deaf since she did not speak until the age of four. Wieck had not only chosen a name for her, meaning 'shining light' or 'famous lady', as his daughter was destined to become – he also wrote her diary for her, in the first person, until she was nineteen years old. The arrival of the young Herr Schumann was an unexpected joy for Clara and her two younger brothers Alwin and Gustav, who were never allowed to play, and never received gifts (Clara Wieck was paid for her achievements). In the evenings he told the children stories of fairies and *Doppelgänger* (Lookalike) in his room, they thought up charades, and he dressed as a ghost to play *Fürchtenmachen* (Frightening) with them, a title he later gave to one of his *Kinderszenen* (Child Scenes) in 1838. *Gespenstermärchen* (Ghost Story), one of the pieces for piano duet for *Children Old And Young*, (Op 85), is a reminder of this time. In 1836 Clara Wieck called the first of her four pieces, Op 5, Le Sabat, or Dance of the Witches, and the last one *Le Ballet des Revenants*, Ballet of the Ghosts. Critics were amazed that a girl so young should compose 'a witches' dance'.[24]

Wieck greatly admired Bach's piano music, in a period when few did, and at the same time he was remarkably receptive to avant-garde music. There were frequent disagreements between Wieck and Schumann during piano lessons – these most often due to the obstinacy of the pupil. By December 1830 Schumann was considering taking lessons from Hummel in Weimar, which Wieck found hurtful. In the summer of 1831 Schumann broke off his piano studies with Wieck. It was not long before *Meister Raro,* as Schumann called him, was renamed *Meister Allesgeld* (Mr Moneybags) for his penny-pinching ways (T1,371). Schumann was increasingly put off by Wieck's arrogance, his *charlatan habits*, his dishonesty (T1,363) and his often tyrannical severity. Yet he missed him when he was away on concert tours with Clara, felt *a void* until he 'had him back' (T1,355,383). In August 1831 he witnessed a scene with Wieck that thoroughly upset him: *Allwin* [sic.] *had not played* [his violin] *properly . . . I cannot tell you how he* [Wieck] *trembled and swayed as he threw him to the floor, pulled his hair, then sat down to rest before renewing his attacks . . . throwing his victim down again, how the little boy begged to be given the violin, he wanted to play, he wanted to play, and all the while Zilia* [one of Schumann's names for Clara] *smiled and sat quietly at the piano with a sonata by Weber* (T1,364).

Schumann worked long and hard during 1831 and 1832. The budding virtuoso took Moscheles as his model, but he still doubted whether he was on the right track. While practising he applied his deepest concentration in finding the most perfect sound[25] (T1,337) and talked to himself as Eusebius: *raise your fingers gently, hold your hand still and play slowly, then everything will come out right again* (T1,349). In October 1831 there were setbacks once more with a temporary *paralysis* in his right hand, and *inner turmoil* (Q78) – should he give up the idea of a career as a virtuoso because of his *shyness in front of an audience* (Jb147). At times he *cried in rage* at his *abominable* playing, and then gave another try to his *cigar method* (T1,354,386). A short time later, on 14 June 1832, it was finally decided that the third finger of his right had was *completely stiff* (T1,410). All attempts to repair the disaster, such as numerous medicines, *herbal poultices, animal baths, hot brandy infusions* (Jb 188), homeopathy and electrical stimulus, were in vain.

Robert Schumann's theory lessons with Heinrich Dorn, the young music director at the Leipzig Court Theatre, included exercises in basso continuo, counterpoint and writing two and three part fugues, but only lasted from July 1831 to Easter 1832. His obstinate pupil often disagreed with Dorn's tone and his views: to Dorn *music is a fugue* (Jb162), but to Schumann that conscious rationality in music *was death* as this allowed *no poetry* (T1,336). Schumann was hurt that Dorn himself called a halt to the lessons, though in retrospect he acknowledged the *good influence* (Jb162) of this teacher. Schumann now practised double counterpoint and fugal writing *in a prosaic and clearheaded manner* using a book by Friedrich Wilhelm Marpurg (T1,408) and set about reading scores and learning instrumentation, using examples from Beethoven. His *grammar* was Bach's *Well-Tempered Clavier* (Jb187). He played the preludes and fugues, mostly as duets, with Glock or with Clara Wieck, then dissected them *one after the other to their very depths* (Jb187), so that they became models for his own compositions. Bach's choral works had been almost forgotten until 1829 when Mendelssohn performed the St Matthew Passion at the Berlin Singakademie. Evidence of a

Bach renaissance can be seen in the much admired 'Historical Soirées' instituted in 1836 by Moscheles in London, and in Mendelssohn's series of historical concerts at the Leipzig Gewandhaus, beginning in 1837.

The first in the new style of poetic compositions for piano that Schumann wrote between 1830 and 1839 was *Papillons*, Op 2. He made veiled references to friends about a connection between this new work and the 'Dance of the Larvae' chapter in Jean Paul's *Flegeljahren* (Walt and Vult): the new cycle was a *musical setting of this dance of the larvae*. He described to Ludwig Rellstab his programmatic titles for the individual pieces in the cycle (Jb167), and for a long time it was thought that the work was in fact programme music,[26] although the manuscript contains no programmatic directions. On the subject of a connection with *Flegeljahre*, Schumann later said that *he adapted the text to the music, rather than the other way around*, and asked Henriette Voigt: *Are the Papillons not clear by themselves?* (NF54) He had *learned more counterpoint* from Jean Paul then he had from his *music teacher*, or so he wrote to a friend (NF149). This cycle of twelve miniatures was the first in a series of dance-scenes and masked balls, continued in *Carnaval*, Op 9, the *Davidsbündlertänze* (David's League Dances), Op 6, *Faschingsschwank* (Carnival Tale), Op 26, *Ballszenen* (Ball Scenes), Op 109 and *Kinderball* (Children's Ball), Op 130. In contrast to Weber's *Invitation to the Dance*, the 12 pieces in *Papillons* were not set within a preconsidered formal framework, but had hidden threads running through them, with quotations or variations on motifs heard earlier in the work. A tonality that sometimes seems to be almost fluffy, a temporarily blurred melodic setting, caused by new parts that are added almost unnoticeably (for example, a *basso cantando* or disturbingly syncopated figures in the accompaniment), all this underlines a character of instability. This is also achieved by the fast changes in harmony and keys and the uneven balance between the different numbers. Contours are blurred by shifted metres, pauses and hesitations act like interrogation marks (Nos 2 and 9). The gradual dissolving of clear periodic structures and figures fluttering out of reach, gives *Papillons* a transitory character. Schumann had made a note in the summer of 1832: *The signature of our time is inconstancy, as we chase after ideas, dreams, opinions and beliefs* (T1,130). He found in *Papillons* the artistic expression for a new experience of time. Social and technical developments were happening so fast, that the passage of time seemed to be shortened, as if time were 'fleeing'.[27] He was portraying a period where the future seemed open, no longer anchored in the past; in which 'experience was a constant surprise', replacing the 'natural ebb and flow'.[28] The image of time fleeing is realised most vividly in the finale of the cycle, where the last waltz, the *Grossvatertanz* (Dance of the Grandfather), is pushed aside by the *Kehraus* (the last traditionally fast dance of a ball), wavers and is gradually broken into tiny fragments as the echo of the final chord fades away: *as if the play had . . . finished, but the curtain did not fall* – Schumann's impression of the conclusion of *Flegeljahre* (NF54).

It was a principle of Romanticism to break down boundaries between the arts, particularly those between music and literature, and so music, where it *inclines towards Romanticism* (T1,361), becomes speech, capable, like literature, of reflecting different levels of consciousness. The guests at a soirée in Wieck's house did not really understand the work; they *could not comprehend the quick transformations* (T1,399). For Wieck himself, who praised the work, there was something exotic about it: he called it *piquant and American* (T1,384). At this period, when 'technical facility, the precision of an automaton . . . was held in the highest regard',[29] the *Étude* and the piano concerto were the preferred forms. Schumann was later to write critically, in the *Neue Zeitschrift für Musik*, on the glitter in Bertini's Etudes, on their *common figures of speech . . . expressed with apparent depth* (GS1,207), and on those of Cramer and Czerny. In his own Concert Studies on Caprices by Paganini, Op 3 and Op 10, Schumann was proposing something of a contrast. He was searching out new expressive possibilities in the sound of his instrument, and also discovering how the concept of *dexterity* could be combined with *expression* (T1,343), demonstrated in such a fascinating way by Paganini. At one point Florestan says that the *proximity of this great man* could bring *him to tears, to laughter, to cheering, to prayer, forgetting all else and swept away in delight* (GS2,272). Many recognised in the virtuoso player the expression of a more elevated existence, a greatness denied to themselves. Where the victory over the greatest technical difficulties was seen as heroic, the virtuoso seemed to personify freedom and independence in the commercialised music business. Only here his 'free' improvisation was regarded as a possible expression of subjectivity, although there were books and lessons that taught how to improvise. Schumann arranged twelve of Paganini's Caprices with accompaniments, performance markings and fingerings; his

Niccolò Paganini. Caricature by Johann Peter Lyser, 1828

extensive introduction and the preparatory technical exercises show how didactic he was. The group of virtuoso works for piano includes, as well as the *Allegro,* Op 8, (intended as the opening movement of a sonata), the *Toccata,* Op 7, a *perpetuum mobile* with the swinging rhythm of a pendulum. It is clear from his figuration how Schumann avoided using the middle finger of his right hand – so he was able perform the piece despite his disability. Its polyphony and the choice of a baroque genre pay homage to Johann Sebastian Bach, while the work also contains elements of the sonata, which in turn interested Sergei Prokofiev, who was inspired by Schumann's Toccata in his own *mobile* pieces.[30]

Schumann had begun work on a Symphony in G minor in October 1832; it promised *the best hope for the future* (NF40), although he was often uncertain about the instrumentation. The first movement, at least, had to be finished fast as there was an opportunity for performance in the middle of November, at one of Clara Wieck's concerts in Zwickau. It was in fact performed on that occasion, though without receiving much attention. The audience was much more interested in hearing Clara play the *Bravura Variations* by Herz. Schumann's work was, nevertheless, his most ambitious yet, as the symphony, alongside opera, was considered the most demanding musical form. So, he continued to work on it after the Zwickau concert – he added a fast scherzo in the slow second movement, but the fugal finale remained a fragment. Its composition shows skill in counterpoint, extended work on the development, unusual modulations and a unity of thematic material. The influence of Beethoven is clear, but this work also shows how Schumann was trying to break free from his overpowering influence by integrating the movements of his symphony. Although Schumann was not yet successful in creating a cycle of movements in this symphony, it expresses nevertheless a new and contemporary feeling that his audience felt to be 'restlessness'. This can be seen immediately in the almost excessive speed of the opening, in the way Schumann avoided symmetry and accepted patterns with his varied reprises, in the principle of developing motifs from previous melodic figures, creating an impression of flow and constant change. The two movements were performed on 29 April in the Leipzig Gewand-haus. In contrast with the *Symphony in C major* by the nineteen-year-old Richard

The first time a work by Schumann (first movement of Symphony in g-minor) was performed was during a concert of Clara Wieck in 1832

Wagner, that had been well-received in January and had received encouraging reviews, the critics commented on the lack of feeling

The concert hall in the Leipzig Gewandhaus. Steel engraving, c. 1845

in Schumann's composition, on the amateur instrumentation and above all on the strange 'restlessness'. The *Allgemeine Musikalische Zeitung* made no mention of the work at all. 'Herr Wagner surpassed you' teased the thirteen-year-old Clara Wieck (L1,55). Schumann must have regarded the indifferent reception of his symphony, for which he had high hopes, as a painful setback. He made no further reference to the work, gave it no opus number, and it was another eight years before he again ventured to write a symphony. He changed the professional description in his passport from 'artist' to 'academic musician'.

Schumann appears to have been almost completely unmoved by the news from Poland, that led to student demonstrations in Leipzig, and by the 'Polish fever' at the beginning of 1832, when exiled Polish freedom fighters entered Leipzig to great public rejoicing. His intense work on his compositions went hand in hand with a growing *discomfort in society*, where he felt himself to be *stiff and dull*. Schumann was always exhorting himself to work, *continually making myself work hard*; he had to stop being *too easily content with mediocrity* (T1,332, 416, 350, 344). While he was composing, even with *all passions suppressed* (Jb145), and *every sensual urge . . . stifled* (T1,391), and if he was leading a *pure, solid and sober life* (Jb144), there nevertheless remained the longing for another sort of happiness: *God! . . . give me just one person I can hold to my heart – a beloved woman* (T1,375). The woman to whom he had been referring in his diary since 1831 either by her first name or as *Charitas*, could not satisfy this longing; Schumann felt guilty as a result of this secret relationship, as if he were *sinking into the mud* (T1,344). It is probable that Schumann contracted syphilis in the summer of 1831. The disease is never named in his diary, but his references indicate social condemnation: Schumann writes of *discoveries, of Nemesis and guilt* (T1,331,330). His doctor only learned of this infection in 1855.[31]

The tensions of 1833 can be seen in Schumann's constant

change of lodgings: he moved out of Wieck's house at the end of 1832, in March he was living with Lühe, in the summer in 'Rudolph's Garden', in September in the Burgstrasse. At the beginning of July 1833, he fell ill with *cold fever*, quite a dangerous form of malaria. The shock of the death of his brother Julius and his sister-in-law Rosalie led to severe depression in the last months of 1833; Schumann was suffering from the *most dreadful melancholy*, and had *a fixed idea* . . . that he was *going mad* (T1,419). During this dark time Ludwig Schuncke appeared *like a star* in December (T1,419). Together they discovered their *Wahlverwandtschaft* (JD 124), (their 'elective affinity'), they moved into rooms together, wrote newspaper articles and dedicated compositions to each other. Then in December 1834 Schuncke died of tuberculosis.

Schumann's aspirations to write a symphony were not completely forgotten, as can be seen from his work, begun in September 1833, on the *Études en forme de variations* (Studies in the Form of Variations), Op 13. At first Schumann called these 12 variations, on a theme he took from the variations of Hauptmann von Fricken, *Etüden im Orchestercharakter* (Studies of an Orchestral Character), then when they were printed in 1837 they became *Études Symphoniques*. Schumann was not writing variations in the style of his time, such as Clara Wieck's *Bellini Variations*, Op 8, but rather his own personal method based on selected elements of the theme. By freeing himself from the form of the theme, he was able to replace the simple sequence of variations with a 'symphonic' development. The aptness of the first title given to the work is clear not only from the 'orchestral' colours he employs – sonority, extremes of register, colour contrasts and polyphonic texture, where the middle voices and the bass state the themes – but also from development-like sections, and the grandiose move from the sombre C sharp minor theme to the triumphant final march in D flat major, that opens with the rising notes of a major triad, a sort of inversion of the beginning of the theme itself. The League of David music is also evident in the sonority and the growing intensity of the music, driven by a single rhythmic motif; this can also be heard in the *Davidsbündlermarsch* (David's League March) of Op 9 (Carnaval), the Scherzo of Op 17 (Fantasia) or later in the Revolutionary Marches, Op 76. Although this music, with its descriptive and symphonic character, was clearly intended for public performance, the cycle also contains another, personal element, shielded from the voices of the outside world – especially in the G sharp minor Etude, No 11, where one voice is answered by a second and their song *quasi a due* soars over boundless depths. The rondo theme of the finale contains a quotation from Marschner's *Der Templer und die Jüdin* (The Templar and the Jewish Woman), 'Proud England rejoice', a tribute to his English friend the composer William Sterndale Bennett, to whom Op 13 is dedicated. Schumann himself realised that the Etudes were unlikely to *appeal to a wide audience* (Bw93) and advised Clara Wieck against a public performance. Even the most virtuoso of the variations, Nos 3, 5, 6 and 9, demonstrate an irritating superficiality rather than bravura writing. Schumann's cycles best suited a new type of concert, inaugurated by Liszt in 1841 – the piano evening.

Schumann had his first *literary achievement* (Jb 151), and first modest success in this field, with an article on Chopin's *Concert Variations*, Op 2, which was published by Fink on 7 December 1831 in the *Allgemeine Musikalische Zeitung*, although the author's name was incorrect ('By K Schumann. Opus II'), and, as a precautionary measure, they printed a second review 'by a highly regarded representative of the old school'[32] alongside. Schumann had played these variations on Mozart's *Là ci darem la mano* from *Don Giovanni* with great enthusiasm in the summer of 1831, and although it was a very early work, composed in 1827 when Chopin was just 17, Schumann could see that this still relatively unknown composer was making a *great leap* in the development of music.

Two completely new personages appeared for the first time in Schumann's article – *Florestan and Eusebius* (T1,344), who bore quite a close resemblance to the twins Walt and Vult in Jean Paul's *Flegeljahre*. Schumann later portrayed them in the music of his *Davidsbündlertänze*, Op 6. Florestan, the *soaring idealist* (GS2,260), whose name was familiar from Beethoven's *Fidelio* and Tieck's *Franz Sternbalds Wanderungen*, was to represent Schumann's *real self in a story* – a novel to be entitled *Florestan* (T1,371). Schumann also gave *more beautiful and appropriate names* to his friends (T1,339).[33] He *took great pleasure in smuggling* his own thoughts into his writing *under pseudonyms* (GS2,261). Schumann's article on Chopin stood out as being particularly unconventional beside the counter review published in the same issue: his spontaneity in *hats off, gentleman – a genius!*, his fictitious brotherhood into which the reader was drawn, and, especially, his way of presenting the music in poetic images or scenes, using characters from *Don Giovanni* – such as Leporello, who *listened behind the bushes, laughing and jeering* (GS1,6). Instead of the solid business of the critic he was portraying a scene where friends were listening to the music together in the evening and talking about it. The critic himself has become a fictional character,

Frédéric Chopin. Drawing by Eugène Delacroix

signing the article as *Julius* (Julius Knorr had played the Variations at the Gewandhaus at the end of September), part of the game between fiction and reality.

At the end of 1833 a number of musicians, mostly from the younger generation, would meet every evening in Leipzig, as if by chance, and almost always in the *Kaffeebaum, young hotheads*, who wanted to *stem the mediocrity* of public musical life (GS1,1,384). And so the *Davidsbund*, an *imaginary league*, was formed, a group of fictitious and real people (Schuncke, Lyser, Banck, Knorr, Rakemann, Heller, Zuccalmaglio, and initially also Wieck) who all had fanciful pseudonyms. Here was the *ideal of a great brotherhood of artists* (GS1,384,383), a 'secret society' as in Jean Paul's *Die unsichtare Loge*,[34] in reality nothing more than a group of friends. In contrast to Carl Maria von Weber's *'Harmonischer Verein'* (Harmonious Society), the Berlin *'Tunnel über der Spree'* (The Tunnel across the Spree) or the Viennese *'Ludlamshöhle'* (Cave of Ludlam) with its rather Biedermeier character, Schumann's League of David came about in reaction to the social isolation of the artist, as the *'Tunnel über der Pleisse'*[35] (Tunnel across the Pleisse) in Leipzig had also done. People were expecting social changes from art and reflection on art. The *Meistersinger* (Mastersinger) had chosen King David with his harp as

Table in coffeehouse 'Kaffeebaum' reserved for the regular meetings of members of the 'David Bond'

their patron saint. Now he became the symbol for *a league to strike the Philistines, both musical and otherwise* (GS2,261). An article in *Der Komet* hinted at all sorts of secret goings-on amongst the members of the League of David – the meetings were said to be reminiscent of the '*Serapionsbrüder*' (Brothers of Serapion) of E T A Hoffmann. The diary entry *Behave in a thoroughly romantic manner!* (T1,339) shows that there was a calculated charm in the myst-ification. The League of David idea appeared in musical form in the piano cycles [*Carnaval*] Op 9 and [*Davidsbündlertänze*] Op 6, but Schumann was not successful in *giving the League of David a real life* and thus escaping his social isolation (NF87). He mostly spent his evenings in the Kaffeebaum, watching silently like the lame observer portrayed by E T A Hoffmann,[36] *often dreaming and brooding deep into the night* (T2,37). Frequently he visited outlying restaurants where no one would recognise him.

In March 1833 Schumann was considering plans to found a journal on the same lines as *Der Komet*, published by his friend Karl Herlossohn. Free criticism was not possible in the existing music journals due to the personal interests of their publishers, who wished to see their own point of view presented, and to set down their own markers in the uncertain political situation. A growing readership over the last fifteen years had demonstrated an increasing need for information, so the undertaking was coming *at a good time and in favourable circumstances* (GS1,383). The Leipzig *Allgemeine Musikalische Zeitung,* published by the best-known music publishers, Breitkopf & Härtel, had the greatest influence, and was highly regarded when Friedrich Rochlitz was its editor. He had been succeeded in 1827 by Gottfried Wilhelm Fink, a theologian who also composed songs and motets. His editing style was so very gentle, in Schumann's opinion, that the *Allgemeine* had sunk to being the 'most general', and was rapidly becoming a *Pantoffelzeitung,* a 'slippers' publication (GS1,284, 164). Soon countless editorials in the *Allgemeine Musikalische Zeitung* were targeting Schumann's journal and the 'Devil's Romantics'. Fink, a bitter opponent of this youthful competition, now never mentioned Schumann's compositions. Then there was Ludwig Rellstag – rather different from Fink – a feared critic, who had twice been arrested for his violent attacks. In his journal *Iris im Gebiete der Tonkunst* (Iris in the Field of Tonal Art), founded in

First edition of the *New Periodical for Music*

1830, he was fiercely opposed to the New Romantics; he considered Chopin's compositions 'deserved to be torn up' (GS1,164), and of the living composers he only rated Cherubini, Spohr, Ludwig Berger and Mendelssohn. One of the few music critics who recognised the progressive qualities in Schumann's music was Gottfried Weber, of the Mainz *Caecilia*.

After much painstaking correspondence to find colleagues and a publisher, the first issue of the *Neue Leipziger Zeitschrift für Musik* appeared on 3 April 1834, produced by Hartmann (a small book publisher), and *edited by a group of artists and friends of the arts* as it was euphemistically put. The founders[37] were in fact four pianists: Schumann, Wieck, Schuncke, and Knorr, who would become the chief editor. A mere three months later Schumann was left to carry the main burden of the enterprise as editor-in-chief – *not what he had been intending* (GS1,383f) Wieck was *perpetually away travelling, Knorr was ill*, and Schuncke had no idea *how to wield a pen* (Jb242); so Schumann had to find new colleagues, including freelance and foreign correspondents,[38] devise projects, write texts, correct proofs and also worry about the finances. There were perpetual problems with Hartmann, so the contract with him was dissolved in December, after much time-consuming negotiation, and in the new year, 1835, publication began with Johann Barth as a bi-weekly journal, with the new title *Neue Zeitschrift für Musik*. Robert Friese took over publication in July 1837. Schumann edited the journal, *really on my own* (Jb240), but with such skill and tenacity that it soon became accepted despite all the problems. *The orderly repetition of such a business* had made Schumann *orderly himself* (Bw137) and at least gave him something firm to hold on to for the moment. Whereas he was shy and withdrawn in close contact with others, the journal gave him a voice with which to speak with enthusiasm, while remaining aloof – impossible for him to do in other circumstances. He worked with *zeal* (Jb242) in the hope of *creating an era where musical education was available to all* (GS1,167) and of laying the groundwork for a *new poetic age* (GS1,38). There was nothing to be expected from the conservatives, the *old brigade*, the *contrapuntalists and antichromaticists* (GS1,144) who sought to *imitate*

Robert Schumann as a student in Leipzig. Reproduction of a missing portrait by an unknown artist, circa 1834

everything ancestral right down to pigtails and periwigs (GS1,159), and certainly there was nothing in the prevailing music business, the *Juste-Milieu*, where *young and old are mixed together* (GS1,144) without direction, and where *the Philistine midgets, restoration cowards all,* have lulled everything to *sleep* (GS1,166). Only *the young men, with their Phrygian bonnets, who despise set forms, and have*

Hector Berlioz. Caricature, 1846

the courage of their own convictions (GS1,144) were advancing the music of the future.

Schumann recognised encouraging signs of this *poetic age* in Chopin and Berlioz, then, later, in Brahms. *The best of the young crowd* (GS1,247) also included William Sterndale Bennett and Adolphe Henselt. Schumann's admiration for Hermann Hirschbach, in whom he saw *much of the Faustian* (GS2,417), similar to himself, was to prove one of his few bad judgements. Although it would have been very important for Schumann to have notices and reviews of his own works, he only referred to them occasionally in his journal – it was intended *for others* (NF84)[39]. He did, however, consider it imperative *to place as heavy an emphasis as possible on old composers and their works* (GS1,37): on the great Bach, the *forerunner of a new era* (GS2,426), and on Beethoven, in whom he saw *moral strength* and *poetic freedom* (GS1,17). He was firmly convinced that the *laws of morality* were also *those of art* (GS2,170), and that music was the *outpouring of a beautiful nature* (GS1,388), while in addition he held the view that life could be changed by raising the profile of education in the arts. He was convinced that such a change would be brought about by Mendelssohn's *oratorio St Paul,* that it would be *the prophet of a beautiful future*, by means of the *deeply*

Felix Mendelssohn. Painting by Wilhelm Hensel, 1844

religious sentiments it embodied and its *masterly music* (GS1,323f), and when he looked back on Leipzig musical life in 1838 there were clear pointers to this future: *striving everywhere, great strength, the worthiest of ambitions* (GS1,380).

Leipzig had become a major centre for music after successfully capturing Felix Mendelssohn to be Kapellmeister of the Gewandhaus in the autumn of 1835. Schumann wrote about the first of the newly inaugurated subscription concerts: *A hundred hearts were turned to him in the first moments*; the only annoyance was the *conductor's baton*, unusual at the time (GS1,117f). Although Mendelssohn kept himself more aloof from Schumann than he did from many other musicians, they did develop a sort of friendship – on Schumann's side a much deeper one than with any other of the Davidsbündler. He looked up to Mendelssohn, who seemed to embody both brilliance and morality, as he would to a *high mountain peak* (NF72). Schumann wrote, in his

Erinnerungen an F Mendelssohn (Memories of Mendelssohn) (p 55), that *his life is a work of art – a perfect one!* Mendelssohn seemed to possess those attributes for which Schumann longed. He was *Felix Meritis*, who seemed effortlessly to achieve success in all fields – he played the piano, the organ and the viola all magnificently, he was a gifted conductor, talented at drawing, was excellently versed in literature and at the age of 16 had composed such a perfect work as the Octet, Op 20, he had an attractive personality, without vanity and he was his own best critic. Schumann was quite aware that Mendelssohn showed little understanding for the music of the avant-garde, that he did not perform Berlioz, showed hardly any interest in Schumann's journalistic work and emphatically rejected poetic criticism – indeed he once wrote that Mendelssohn could well learn *something* from him (Jb283).

Schumann devoted a great deal of time to the works of contemporary composers, even those who were completely insignificant. He read with care, criticised helpfully and suggested amendments, was *extremely hard* (GS1,429) particularly on the best pieces, and gave advice and encouragement. In his youth he was an excellent teacher. Later he would fail in front of the pupils at the conservatory. His journal was also intended to assist the large number of amateur musicians, and so he was advocating the use of titles and performance markings in German, and German music generally. Concerts at the time were dominated by French virtuoso pieces, and Italian opera. There ought to be a *polemical school* of critics who would *take a courageous stance* – criticism as *passage at arms* (GS1,29,222), to set new standards, to do battle with *the supremacy of the fashionable and the philistine, with the false pathos and artificial profundity* of the virtuoso, with music degraded as a commodity by *awful talents and mass producers*, who only compose *for money* (GS1,179,155, 38,96); and to fight against the susceptibility of German music to the Italian influence, that causes a *weak and soft character*

(GS1,150). For this reason it was vital to dislodge the so-called *German-Italian school*, with its melodies set to triplet accompaniments and their consumptive suspensions and to tear down the *foreign idols*. Schumann had particular fun mocking the piano virtuoso Henri Herz, who was *most airily elegant and never lifted a finger except to play and most importantly to hold on to his money and his reputation* (GS1,297,383,153). An example of how this polemical enlightenment could strike out in blind denunciation can be seen in Schumann's savage criticism of Meyerbeer's *Huguenots*, premiered in Paris in 1836, and performed the following year in Leipzig – its quotation of the chorale *Ein' feste Burg* (A Firm Castle) amounted to a profanation of the most holy in art. Schumann argued in a madly nationalistic and provincial fashion that what he saw here was quintessentially *common, distorted, unnatural, uncouth, unmusical,* an example of the *distortion of the times* (GS1,321,323).

Schumann did, however, promote foreign artists such as Chopin, Berlioz, Liszt, Heller and Sterndale Bennett, and he appreciated the works of the *fine* Italian composer Cherubini (GS1,339). Convinced as he was about the autonomy of works of art, he sought to wean the public away from the culinary to an understanding of a different form of art. *Florestan's Fastnachtsrede* is just such a public scolding, a nasty satire on the audience for Beethoven's Ninth symphony, on musical philistines who feel in sympathy with artists and works – even laying claim to them themselves – as substitutes for something they themselves cannot do. On the other hand, amateurs, in the true sense of the word, were always encouraged *not to fear too much from the professionals* (GS1,175), while Schumann repeatedly recommended simpler pieces that could be played at home, persuaded of the *mutual benefit* both for art and for the amateur performer (GS1,112).

Schumann was of the opinion that criticism could only be levelled at a musical work when it had ceased to be analytical and *petty-minded* (GS1,77), and had itself been turned into poetry.[40] This led to various literary forms of musical criticism in the *Neue Zeitschrift,* often in the style of Jean Paul: fictitious letters, narrative and literary interpretations, satires and aphorisms. Schumann thought that the *highest level of criticism was that which itself conveys the impression that was created by the original* (GS1,44). His extended review of Berlioz's *Symphony fantastique* shows, however, that sometimes *detailed analysis* was necessary to counter the opponents of this 'poetic' criticism.[41] Schumann found that his aim of educating his reader was best achieved with criticism in the form of a dialogue, or by parallel reviews, that is, criticism from various different points of view, so that the reader could follow opposing arguments and form his own judgement. This enabled him to present extremes, with over-exaggeration – particularly when the *hothead* Florestan (GS1,165) *could immediately sense the deficiency in a work* where *Eusebius with his gentler side* could *often overlook the faults* in a piece because of its *beauties* (GS1,60). The arguments were not always between fictional figures – differing points of view were quite often presented. By March 1838 the journal had 450 subscribers, and was as dear to Schumann as a tree he had planted himself, but it still did not represent what he amongst *so many millions had been chosen to do* (Bw247).

A Life in Letters

Schumann watched Clara Wieck from a distance, but with increasing interest: her silly behaviour and her moods, her *childlike originality* (T1,383), her wild streak and her *enormous passion* (T1,334). At the end of September 1831, Wieck and his daughter set off on a tour to Paris from which they only returned in May of the following year – with a medal Goethe had presented to 'the gifted artist Clara Wieck'. Schumann remarked that she was *prettier* and *more adept*, that she spoke with a French accent and played *like a hussar* (T1,383). She studied his enormously difficult *Etudes, Op 3*, and played two of them for his birthday. She had composed several piano pieces herself, dances and variations, and most recently a *Romance Variée*, a set of brilliant variations in the contemporary style that she dedicated to Schumann. He in turn took the theme for his *Impromptus sur une Romance de Clara Wieck, Op 5*, from these variations. This inaugurated a sort of musical correspondence between the two of them, continued in Schumann's sonatas Op 11 and Op 14, in the *Davidsbündlertänzer, Op 6*, the eighth *Novellette, Op 21*, and in Clara Schumann's Fugues, Op 16 and her Sonata in G minor. In Schumann's *Impromptus* Clara's theme has a bass line in unison at first. The title 'Impromptus' rather than 'Variations' is an example of the new style of variations Schumann had first used in his Op 1; the theme is not always evident, but it appears as a *memory*, as here in the bass (GS1,222), recurring in various ways throughout the variations: hidden in the middle voices, reduced to fragments, intervals or harmonic sequences. Schumann's intensive studies of Bach can be seen in the passacaglia-like writing of the bass, and in the four-part fugue of the finale. The Intermezzi, Op 4, also show the influence of Bach with the baroque style of melody in the fugato. Like *Papillons*, they show a literary influence, being described as 'leaves from a diary',[42] *an opera without a text* (T1,412). In the second intermezzo the libretto of this opera seemed to be reduced to one fragment: *Meine Ruh' ist hin* (My peace is gone).

Clara Wieck. Lithograph by Eduard Clemens Fechner, 1832

Schumann later wrote that he had *long known* (Bw20) what Clara was unconsciously saying in her letters to 'Herrn Schumann', with their childish provocation, their playfulness, and in the shy dedication of a 'trifle', such as her Romance, Op 3. In 1833 letters went backwards and forwards between their two houses, even though the 14-year-old could often only decipher Schumann's writing 'with the help of her mother [stepmother]' (Bw7). The following year, when Wieck sent his daughter to Dresden to study theory and singing with Reissiger and Mieksch, respectively Hofkapellmeister and Choirmaster there, a new piano pupil moved into the Wieck household: Ernestine von Fricken who came from Asch – a young woman when compared with Clara Wieck who was three years younger: *The daughter of a rich baron from Bohemia . . . a wonderfully pure and childlike disposition, gentle and thoughtful . . . extremely musical – in short, exactly the sort of person I would seek as a wife,* Schumann wrote in a letter to his mother (Jb243). They were secretly engaged in August, but the *summer novel* (Jb256) lasted less than a year. Schumann felt that he had been kept too long in the dark about the *poverty* and the *unfortunate family circumstances* (Bw96) of the young woman, who was only an adopted daughter of the baron, and for this reason would not inherit. His relationship with Ernestine von Fricken later became one of friendship, as can be seen from the works he dedicated to her, Op 8 and Op 31. The *summer novel* found musical expression in the cycle *Carnaval*, Op 9, written in 1834-35. The tone-row ASCH (in German terminology AS = A flat; S = E flat; H = B natural), often repeated in the composition, denotes both the place from which Ernestine von Fricken came and the setting of an imaginary festivity, and is at the same time the musical representation of his own name SCHumAnn.

The introduction, like an overture and grandly marked quasi maestoso, indicates a drama, and its fast final section returns at the end to make a frame for the whole cycle. The players are Davidsbündler: Florestan, Eusebius, Chiarina (Clara Wieck), Estrella (Ernestine von Fricken), Chopin, Paganini, Schubert and Beethoven, sometimes hidden behind masks borrowed from the *Commedia dell'arte*. Against the background of various dances are scenes of dialogue: gentle conversations (*Aveu, Reconnaissance, Réplique*) (Confession, Recognition, Reply), a little dispute

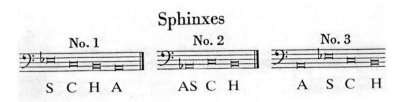

Sphinxes from *Carnaval* op. 9

(*Pantalon et Colombine*) – an excited buffo-like chattering with a suitable reconciliation (*dolce*) – there is even a monologue (*Eusebius*). Schumann was experimenting with a new type of variation: with the exception of the introduction,[43] each section contains the tone-row ASCH in a different form. Only *Chopin* has a variant of it. The meaning of *Sphinxes* seems as open to various interpretations as the cipher itself – here at the centre of the cycle the combination of notes appears in breves.

They indicate the coded identity, but at the same time they are like moths, formless as they emerge from their cocoon, gradually revealing themselves. The masks in *Carnaval* appear like the dreams of another fictional self. The cycle's central character is *Florestan*.[44] His portrait, containing a quotation from *Papillons* – a motto in flashback for the set – is not fully sketched, and as his motif disintegrates the piece ends in dissonance, a question awaiting its answer. *Pierrot* leads the cast of characters, with a *melancholy* motif (NF57); he is an early forerunner of Stravinsky's poor Petruschka, as can be seen from the incongruity between this sad and desolate puppet and the stereotype of his continually stumbling motif. Other characters appear: the capers of *Arlequin* and *Coquette*, whose dance is driven by a mechanical device (stark fortissimo notes) like the song of the 'automatons' in E T A Hoffmann.[45] The similarity in these motifs shows that *Florestan* is lurking behind this and other masks. Schumann created an enigma in *Chopin*, with references to Chopin's Etude, Op 10 No 9, and a self-portrait in the variant row S, C, B flat, A. He is creating introspective and imaginary visions, acting out scenes whose unreality is displayed in both harmonic and rhythmic alienation. The music of the *Promenade* appears to be sometimes nearer, sometimes more distant, as if passing through several rooms, revealing how Schumann used the spatial element as a structural component in composition, fifty years before Mahler. The march of the Davidsbündler in the finale, steps out of line in triple time and at ever increasing speed, makes a mockery of marching in step; running turns to jumping, and finally leaping into the air, as if the Davidsbündler were flying off like Giannozzo in Jean Paul's airship – into the 'open air of freedom'.[46] Beethoven is also worked into the march of the Davidsbündler with a quotation from his Piano Concerto in E flat major (Finale, bar 25 ff), used in counterpoint with the *Grossvatertanz*, representing the Philistines, perpetually behind the times, they are simply swept along with the power and speed – a utopian vision where battles need no longer be fought.

Clara Wieck returned to Leipzig with her father at the beginning of April 1835 from an exhausting and not entirely successful concert tour that had lasted more than five months. To Schumann she seemed *even more distant and remote* (Bw96), but when he was staying in Zwickau in the late autumn they resumed their correspondence. Friedrich Wieck was aware of their love, their fleeting happiness during the last months of 1835. In January he dispatched his daughter to Dresden, but when he discovered that Schumann had followed her, he forbade him entry to his house, and permitted no letters either. Schumann was deeply hurt by this unexpected animosity from the man who had been like a father to

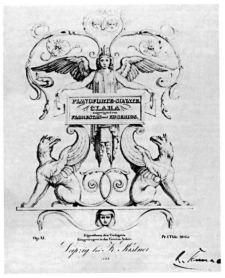

Title page of the first edition of op. 11, drawn by Bonaventura Genelli Schumann's first sonata was *dedicated to Clara by Florestan and Eusebius*

him. When he learned of his mother's death on 4 February, he was again overcome by his old fear of being abandoned, a fear which could only be fought with coldness and rigidity. Schumann drank heavily and could only gradually resume his work. He occasionally saw Clara Wieck from afar, *suffering and very beautiful* (T2,30); his *lament* for her was expressed in the *Fantasie* Op 17 (Jb278). The beginning of the following year, when he *forced himself to try to forget Clara*, seemed his *darkest hour* (Bw67). She was away for months on end on concert tours to Berlin, Hamburg and Dresden, where she played her new Bellini Variations, Op 8 – from memory, which seemed downright immodest to Bettina von Arnim – while Schumann, *with a deadly fear in his heart*, was afraid of losing every support, he was so *dizzy* as he thought of the future (NF83).

After they had been unable to speak or write to one another for more than a year, he sent Clara his F sharp minor Sonata, in May 1837. The key of this work demonstrated its special character, while the title: 'Piano Sonata, Op 11, dedicated to Clara by Florestan and Eusebius', naming the dedicatee only with her first name, was a confession in itself. The composer was hiding behind a double mask, recognisable only to a close circle. The music here finds a *language* to express *the state of the soul* (GS1,22), starting in the introduction with a quotation from one of his early songs (*An Anna*). The lines *Denk' ich dein, du süsses Leben* (I think of you, my sweet life) are quoted in bars 33 ff – in the song these are the words of a dying man to his distant beloved – the quotation returns in the main movement of the sonata (bars 160 ff and 403 ff), the song is finally quoted in full in the slow movement, and is hinted at also in the trio of the scherzo (bars 51–53), in this way the autobiographical becomes a structural element. Memory rising over pain is audible in the introduction, in an imaginary dialogue between a low and a high voice. The principle of dialogue is evident in the aria, and appears in a different form in the exposition, in the opposition of two motifs representing the first theme of the sonata, a *fandango* with pulsing unrest, and a percussion-like bass, a distorted quotation from Clara's Op 5 No 4, identifying the imaginary partner in the dialogue that is the nucleus of the whole cycle: as a falling fifth in the introduction, a falling double fifth in the *aria*, augmented to a falling octave in the scherzo and in yet another guise in the *marcato* motif of the final movement. The subjective character of this work – its free *unfettered speech* (GS1,43), its confessional nature, its deviation from traditional form, especially in the scherzo – these were deliberate aesthetic moves: a protest against the traditional *Mezzoforte* and the *classic-romantic somnolence of the Juste-Milieuistes* (GS1,15,9,103). The finale, where the main themes from the first movement appear once again, demonstrates particularly well how Schumann was trying *to make links and connections, and to unify contrasts* (GS1,250). Yet Moscheles was not alone in thinking that this final movement with its countless different moods, made him think that he was hearing 'division but no reconciliation' (A 137).

The long gestation period of the two remaining sonatas and the Fantasia, Op 17, show how Schumann doubted whether he was not merely a *latecomer from a previous age* in his choice of sonata form. In 1839 he wrote that the sonata had really *run its allotted course* (GS1,306,395). The second movement of the Sonata in G minor, Op 22, contains variations on the song composed in 1828, *Im Herbste* (In Autumn); two further movements were written in 1835, the finale not until 1838. The subjective tone of this work can be seen in the extreme tempo markings: *As fast as possible – faster – even faster* in the first movement, *very fast* in the scherzo, *Presto – prestissimo – ever faster and faster* in the rondo finale. This seemed even to Clara to be 'just too difficult' (Bw108), so Schumann changed it. The Third Sonata, in F minor,

Op 14, completed in 1836, is even more strange with its free use of sonata form and its monothematic nature. In the title *Concert sans orchestre*, Schumann bowed to the wishes of his publisher, Haslinger, who suggested the work should be shortened by two movements. Schumann only reinstated one of its two scherzi in the edition of 1853. An *andantino* by Clara is taken as the theme for the set of variations that form both the motto and the core of the whole cycle. Individual elements of this theme (repeated notes, dotted rhythms) are the basis for almost all the themes and motifs of the sonata – Schumann confessed it was *one single cry from the heart* for Clara Wieck (Bw 104).

Schumann completed his Fantasia, Op 17, in 1838. He had sketched this two years earlier as a *Grand Sonata*, with various titles such as *Ruins, Trophies, Palms,* or *Ruins, Triumphal Arch and Constellation*, but it would burst the framework of a sonata. The proceeds from this composition were originally intended to fund the building of a memorial to Beethoven. The three movements were *Poetry*, free speech in music (Bw145), with a motto at the head in a verse by Friedrich Schlegel: 'In all the tones that echo through earth's bright dream, there is one gentle long-drawn tone for the secret listener', while a quotation from Beethoven's song cycle *An die ferne Geliebte* (To the Distant Beloved) *'Nimm sie hin denn, diese Lieder'* (Accept them, these songs), underlies the whole of the first movement, continually hinted at, then revealed right at the end in the key of C major. *It is you in the 'tone' of the motto, isn't it?* Schumann wrote to Clara (Bw562), on whose *Andantino* the main theme is based, and then again, *the first movement is the most passionate composition that I have ever written – a deep lament for you* (Jb278). When the many links between the main theme and the subsidiary theme, initially presented as classical contrasts, are brought closer and closer together, until they are finally united, an idea becomes an aesthetic form that could never be caught up with reality (bar 101 ff). The first movement signals a departure from classical sonata form, since Schumann was cutting *new paths*, continually transforming what was previously heard, and using speech-like patterns – for example, in the passionate main theme, introduced with the highest note of the chord of the dominant ninth over a deeper underlying sound, in his use of rubato, in the recitative passages, in the contemplative section marked *Legendenton* (in the manner of a legend). This piano music, with its tonal ambiguities, and the diffuse harmonic ground from which the melodies rise, approaches that *wonderful region* Schumann would later discover in Brahms (GS2,301). Liszt, to whom the *Fantasia* is dedicated, said of the conclusion to the first movement, 'These twenty bars are out of this world'.[47]

From 1836 to 1840 Schumann lived in a house at the rear of the 'Rote Kolleg', as a lodger of Frau Devrient. He could look out from his 'peaceful and secluded' rooms onto 'the part of the Promenade surrounding Leipzig that has the most trees and shrubs' (JD60). New works were studied at quartet matinées with the concert master Ferdinand David in a music room hung with portraits of Bach, Beethoven, Ludwig Schuncke and Clara Wieck. At midday in the Hotel de Bavière he often met Mendelssohn, Sterndale Bennett, David, and Walther von Goethe, the grandson of the poet. Other occasional guests might include Lipinski, the concert master from Dresden to whom *Carnaval* was dedicated, or Adalbert von Chamisso, the author of the cycle of poems *Frauenliebe und-leben* (Women's Love-and-Life) that Schumann set in 1840. The others noticed how Schumann was restricting himself to a decreasing circle of friends, and that his conversations were 'ever more broken and abrupt' (E1,109) 'as if he were talking to himself' (W 500). David invited him more frequently to soirées with Mendelssohn, with the violinist Henri Vieuxtemps and with the young English soprano Clara Novello. He was an almost daily guest of the music-loving Voigts, to whom Schunke had introduced him in 1834. Henriette Voigt, a pianist herself, who corresponded with numerous well-known musicians, was one of the women on whose strength Schumann believed he could rely. He *no longer had any woman to protect him*, he wrote to his sister-in-law Therese Schumann, with whom he felt *safe*; as for Clara Wieck, he was *completely resigned* (NF72,71,82). Henriette Voigt became for him *an A flat major soul* (NF56), often *giving advice* and *always loving and kind*, an *Eleonore*; he needed such *Amazons* (NF121) who loved his work and would promote it and protect him from the publicity by which he sometimes felt threatened. Although he saw quite clearly that his piano music was not suited to the concert hall, he still longed for a success that *would make his audience climb the walls in delight* (Bw127). He was still suffering from abrupt mood swings; after the first dark months of the year he suddenly found he could compose *with a bliss* he had *never experienced before*; he wrote the *Fantasiestücke*, Op 12, and the *Davidsbündlertänze*, Op 6 and noted happily: *everything comes out right* (T2,34).

In the *Davidsbündlertänze* Schumann drew pictures of himself as a person he could not present to the real world. Sometimes he added words to the portraits signed F or E, like remnants of a lost prose text. They seemed to indicate a further dimension to the music, evident also in the reflective openings to many of the pieces. The cycle contains pictures of Florestan, the 'poet', who can be identified in the *Ballade* No 10 and the quotation from *Carnaval*; there are pictures of his impulsiveness, his strength and his impatience, shown in syncopated rhythms, swiftly moving bass lines, in the violence of closely placed dissonances and sharp accents (No 4), and in restless harmonies, that reach the tonic at the very last moment (No 9). There are pictures of his obsessive nature (No 6), but also of his humour, where his laughter brushes away everyday problems (No 12). In contrast to these there are portraits of Eusebius, pictures of longing indicated with suspensions and falling semitones; musical monologues; songs dreaming of happiness coming *from a distant place*. Just one year later Schumann no longer *found any trace of Eusebius* in himself (Bw223), but the pieces signed here with F and E demonstrate a unity in which opposites are reconciled (Nos 13, 15, 16/17). The cycle is prefaced with a motto taken from the first bars of a Mazurka from Clara Wieck's *Soirées Musicales*, Op 6, themselves influenced by Chopin. Schumann took them as a departure point in Florestan mode. In these eighteen pieces he was again creating his own form: the cycle is in two symmetrical parts, each with an epilogue, a sort of personal commentary at the end of the section. Connections are made within the cycle through the many transformations of single elements of the motto, repeated like a dream in the lowest register at the conclusion of the cycle. The key structure also creates references within the pieces: for instance, B major, as the most remote from the home key of C major, signifies a different, nocturnal time, as in the deep droning effect at the beginning of No 17, and the strokes of midnight in the last piece; it also indicates distance, where the single notes seem to lose a real dimension, as in the song *Schöne Fremde* (Beautiful Stranger), Op 39 No 6, also in B major, *Es redet trunken die Ferne/wie von künftigem grossen Glück* (the distance speaks rapturously of great happiness to come).

The eight *Fantasiestücke* Op 12, to which Schumann later gave titles that would have been equally suitable for songs or poems, (*Des Abends – Warum? – Traumes – Wirren*) (In the Evening – Why? – Of Dreams – Confusion), are unified by their nocturnal mood. The fifth of these, *In der Nacht* (In the Night), was a particular favourite of Schumann's. He saw in it the story of Leander who *swam across the sea every night to his beloved Hero: first he plunges into the sea – she calls – he replies – he steps happily from the waves onto the land – now the cantilene where they embrace – then, when he must leave, they cannot tear themselves apart – until night once more shrouds everything in darkness* (Bw154). The image of the man swimming at night over the unknown deep goes beyond the personal to stand as a metaphor for living in this age of transition, expressing itself musically in figures that appear in the restless semiquavers, disappear again and have no substance; even the song contained in the more peaceful central section, with its obstinately repeated dissonances, sounds as if it did not fit its harmonic setting. Schumann's achievement in composing this nocturne can be seen in the bold harmonies, especially in the central section, and in his technique of developing music out of the smallest of elements, here the falling semitone.

Clara gave no answer to the sonata Schumann had dedicated to her. Her silence, and the comments of his colleague Carl Banck, who had been Clara's singing teacher since the end of May 1836, and temporarily appeared to be his rival, all added to Schumann's unease and seemed to cripple him. Clara herself took the initiative in renewing contact between them when she finally returned to Leipzig on 5 August 1837. She played her own *Variations*, Op 8, and three of his *Etudes symphoniques*, Op 13, at a concert in the Börsensaal, and to him her playing seemed *as if it were the most perfect one could imagine* (Bw98f). After this matinée they resumed their secret correspondence, and continued writing letters to each other until their marriage in 1840. For Robert Schumann and Clara Wieck this was almost the only form of communication possible, although they lived merely a couple of streets from each other in Leipzig. From now on they celebrated St Eusebius day, 14 August, as the anniversary of their engagement. Schumann wrote formally to ask for Clara's hand, in a letter she gave to her father personally on her eighteenth birthday. Schumann referred proudly to his secure financial situation and to his increasing influence and recognition through his journalism (L1,124). He had accepted the eighteen months of separation from Clara as a test, and he would have subjected himself to a further separation in order to win Wieck's trust. The interview which followed was

Programm

der musikal. Morgenunterhaltung,

g e g e b e n   v o n

Clara Wieck

im Saale der Buchhändlerbörse,

Sonntag am 13. Aug. 183?

Erster Theil.

1) Quartett für 4 Männerstimmen.
2) Lied: „Herein" von Keil, componirt von F. Steg-
   meier, vorgetragen von der königl. sächsischer-
   schen Hofsängerin Fräulein Franchetti.
3) Divertissement über die Cavatine von Pacini:
   „I tuoi frequenti palpiti" von Liszt (Op. 5.),
   gespielt von der Concertgeberin.
4) Zwei Lieder von Reissiger, vorgetragen vom
   Herrn Kammersänger Krüger aus Dessau.
5) Gedicht, gesprochen von Fräulein Marie Wolf.
6) Drei „Etudes Symphoniques," nebst vorhergeh.
   Thema (aus Op. 13.) von Robert Schumann,
       Notturno (H dur) von Chopin,
       Andante und Allegro v. Adolph Henselt,
   sämmtlich vorgetragen von Clara Wieck.

Zweiter Theil.

7) Quartett für 4 Männerstimmen.
8) „Suleika" und „das Veilchen" von F. Men-
   delssohn-Bartholdy, vorgetragen von Fräulein Auguste Werner.
9) Zwei Etuden. Die Erste in Fis dur mit dem
   Motto: „Wenn ich ein Vöglein wär' flög ich zu
   dir." Die Zweite in Es moll, v. Adolph Henselt, gespielt von Clara Wieck.
10) Zwei Lieder: „Es ist ein Reif gefallen" von
    Reiniger, und „Ihre Augen" von Lassmann,
    comp. v. Stegmeier, u. vorgetr. v. Hrn. Swo-
    boda, Mitglied des hiesigen Stadttheaters.
11) Concert-Variationen über die Cavatine aus
    Bellini's Oper: „der Pirat," componirt und
    gespielt von der Concertgeberin.

---

*Billets zu 12 Gr. sind bis Sonnabend Abend in den
Musikhandl. der Herren Hofmeister und Kistner
und in der Wohnung der Concertgeberin (Nicolai-
strasse Nr. 555) zu haben.   An der Casse kostet das
Billet 16 Gr.*

Anfang 11 Uhr.   Ende gegen 1 Uhr.

Programme notes of a Clara Wieck concert

terrible — Schumann had not expected such *coldness*. He was *shaken to his very core* (Bw24,26). Schumann had not fully recovered from his feeling of dislocation following the death of his father, so his *attachment* to the man whom he would *so much have liked to call Father* made him particularly vulnerable to Wieck's animosity (Bw64,118). Wieck opposed the marriage as forcefully as possible, for he feared losing all that he had invested in his daughter's career, and with it his own downfall from a position that meant everything to him — he had experienced sufficient humiliations when he was a tutor. He fought both openly and behind the scenes, with an aggression that was sometimes ludicrous; he attempted to denigrate Schumann with slanders, was not above *common gossip, rumour-mongering and intrigues* and watched for *any false move* on Schumann's part (Bw169, 150); then, when it seemed advantageous, he would suddenly act towards him *with great gentleness and cordiality* (NF96), but he still insisted on the impossible condition — an annual income of 2,000 guilders. On 15 October he set off with his daughter on a seven-month tour to Vienna and despite Clara's great success he could not bridle his anger with his daughter, who now had to fight her father and teacher, whom she loved and honoured, 'for life and death', perpetually fearing an absolute repudiation (Bw132,191).

Writing letters to each other, the only way they could exchange intimacies, meant for both of them uncertainty, waiting, fear of discovery and humiliation when they were dependent on the help of others, such as the lawyer and music-lover Becker or the Leipzig doctor Reuter — both later to be witnesses at their wedding. Schumann wrote to her *poste restante* using a coded address, since Wieck watched the post offices. If his daughter was already known there, then he had to send his letters via a third party. She was constantly afraid that Wieck would catch her writing. Schumann had to read her reports of 'playing courtier': of daily visits from Prince Schönburg and all the other 'lovelorn suitors' in Vienna, of the 'heartfelt sighs' of Louis Rakemann, and the dubious promises of Dr Schilling, who was intriguing against Schumann (Bw44,114, 214). All these stories, however, did not unsettle Schumann as much as Clara's attempt to postpone the date they had agreed for their marriage, when, under her father's influence once more, she demanded that Schumann test himself to see whether he could

Clara Wieck. Water colour and pencil drawing by Elwine von Leyser, 1836

really settle her in 'a worry-free situation'; 'love' was 'all very well, but . . .' if their financial circumstances were not secure 'we would both, as artists, be drowned by worries' (Bw46,511). The journal gave Schumann a measure of support, but he was far from feeling firm ground beneath his feet, and *clung* to this young woman as if their marriage would save him, *a man whose depression was verging on illness,* from plunging into an *immeasurable void* (Bw34,33,71). Klärchen's words in [Goethe's play] *Egmont,* 'Help, dear people, help, help' rang in his head, but those in his letters to Clara were his own cries for help. *He saw her as a girl within her own armour* who might be able to *heal him completely* from his *mental illness* (Bw67,74,185). He dared to write of this to her, although he realised how far apart they really were: *You scarcely know who I am; sometimes I could scream with pain* (Bw232). He tormented himself with feelings of guilt, with the thoughts that he did not *deserve* Clara, especially since she had been made a Royal and Imperial Chamber Virtuoso; Schumann tormented himself with *doubts* about his own capabilities (Bw65,64) and regarded sexuality as a trial to which *he would not be equal* (T2,38). Moral demands and social prejudice had always been bound up with his image of his mother. The fear had remained after her death: *I feel exactly as if my mother had seen me and everything were out in the open* (T2,38). His tendency towards self destruction was evident again in his recurring dreams of drowning, dreams of a *longing to throw himself into the Rhine* (T1,236), into *deep water* or into the *Danube* (Bw48, 154). He forced himself to carry on, exerting permanent self-control, with the determination to be *strong as iron* (Bw202). He suppressed his feelings by constantly working, compositions and music, as for example in the second of the *Fantasiestücke*, the 'upswing' came from his own efforts.

Schumann had had an *idea for a poetic biography of Hoffmann* as early as 1831 (T1,336). *Kreisleriana*, Op 16, written in 1838 is even more closely based on Hoffmann's work than the *Fantasiestücke* and the *Nachtstücke* had been – in this case on the figure of the Kapellmeister Kreisler, in whose 'sufferings' Schumann saw mirrored his own. This fantasy, explicitly named in Schumann's subtitle, had, like its literary antecedents (*Kreisleriana, Lebensansichten des Katers Murr*) (the Cat Murr's View of Life), a mutability inherent in its visionary character. This explains the sketchy, incomplete nature of the music which is light and free throughout (for example, the bass in the last piece), an attempt to make the possible visible. A 'crazy, crazy apparition'[48] is portrayed in the music, a world that might disintegrate at any moment, with the individual fearful that he might lose his balance and sense of direction. On the other hand, these pieces also represent a measure of moderation and security in their references to the past; it is in this interplay that many of the alternations appear as 'a fatal leap from one extreme to the other'.[49] At one extreme, tension is maintained throughout: in the first piece where the melody is just vaguely sketched, with 'delayed' bass notes and triplets in the right hand that seem to drift apart; in the shadowy third piece with its wild climax; in the seventh with its dissonant bass notes, played 'at furious speed' by interpreters such as Vladimir Horowitz, or in the eeriness of the last piece. The opposite extreme can be heard in echoes of music from the past: the balance and clarity of the second piece with its *wonderfully intricate* polyphony (Bw138), that seems so distant, especially when the reprise comes in the remote key of F sharp major in place of B flat major (T131 ff); again, in the fourth piece where the improvisation is presented as reflection, a dream of what might be. Just as Kreisler continued from where the *Goldberg Variations* left off, so Schumann's music reflects his own understanding of Bach, as in the prelude-like second part of the fourth piece and in the rushing fugato of the seventh with its chorale-like ending; further examples are the shadowy gigue at the end, and in the sixth piece, where echoes of Bach appear in an alienated context – subdued in the middle voices – in a music that resembles an ancient folk melody. According to Schumann, *the deep combinations, the poetic and humorous nature of contemporary music* had its *foundation . . . in Bach* (NF177). Although on the one hand the form itself seems to be unbalanced in its improvisatory nature, in its metric and harmonic instability, and in its impetuous opening and the lack of a clear conclusion (the cycle ends with a scarcely audible bottom G), nevertheless on the material level it does constitute an entity, using the smallest of possible opening intervals – a second and a third – repeated almost obsessively, and in variations of many sorts.

Kreisleriana was *dedicated to his friend F Chopin* by Schumann. Chopin replied with the dedication of his F major Ballade, Op 38, '*à Monsieur Schumann*'. He rather disliked Schumann's compositions, though he was coolly polite, and several months passed before he even looked at *Kreisleriana*. Schumann, however, considered it to be one of his *best* piano compositions, an opinion he maintained: a work which was *thought-provoking* (NF227,119).

Schumann described his *Kinderszenen*, Op 15, to Clara as a contrast to *Kreisleriana* – these pieces *resembled* their *future* together: *gentle and loving and happy* (Bw219). They spoke of a 'remembered future' and about the longing for an illusionary childhood where no one has actually ever been.[50] And just as the child embodies the person wishing for something (*The Pleading Child*), so the second part of the *Important Event* alludes to the festival of Christmas in the song 'Tomorrow, children, there will be something for you'. The first piece, the dream *Of Strange Lands and People* with its musical formulation for wishing, the recurrent rising sixth, is the structural model for the whole cycle. *The Poet* in the free recitative of the Epilogue, quoting the two first bars from *Upswing* in the *Fantasiestücke*, indicates where wishes may lead. The high level of organisation in the material of these pieces, the unity of keys and motifs, and the various allusions, such as the BACH motif of the first piece (bars 1–3), the references in the scherzo and adagio movements (Nos 9 and 10), are not immediately obvious. Alban Berg[51] has pointed out the artifice of the polyphony of *Träumerei*, which of all Schumann's pieces has been the most trivialised, countering Pfitzner's argument that *Träumerie* is beyond all reasoning.

Clara 'could not forget' the *Kinderszenen*; 'your beautiful melodies are constantly singing in my head', she wrote in a letter from Paris (Bw491). Schumann often wrote to her of his dreams for the future, of the years when *everything will have a happy end* (Bw188). Perhaps they would live in Vienna, home to Beethoven and Schubert, where they could live in privacy, shielded from increasingly nasty publicity. Sometimes they wanted to travel the world, then return *heaped with riches to the dreamlike seclusion* of their home, to live *quietly* together and *to compose the most magnificent operas* (Bw 49, 70, 51).

Clara Wieck. Lithograph by Andreas Staub, 1838, at the time of her triumphant success in Vienna. Robert Schumann wrote to Clara about this picture and the artist in April 1839: 'I might be afraid of him, since he has seen so deep into your heart.'

Schumann was imagining that his marriage would result in the creation of a lifework together, long before their joint project, *Liebesfrühling*, Op 37.

At the beginning of February 1939 Schumann told Clara of a new work in which she would particularly feature. He had not named it *Wiecketten*, as that did not sound *good enough* (Bw90), but *Novelletten*, after the English soprano, Clara Novello. Schumann added that he had composed *larger-scale, inter-connected adventure stories* (NF118), resembling 'Novellen' in the freedom of their different musical constructions, in their variety and their many references, and also in the indication, occurring twice in the last piece, *continuation*. He published the Intermezzo from the third piece, described in his diary as *Macbeth-Novellette* (T2,50),

Robert Schumann the year before his marriage with Clara. Lithograph by Josef Kriehuber, 1839

as a supplement in the *Neue Zeitschrift*, and set the witches' first couplet from Shakespeare's play over it. The second *Novellette* referred to lines from Goethe's *Der west-östliche Divan* (The west-to-east Divan), possibly the ones he wrote out for Clara; 'There is great joy in being alive!'[52] (Jb284). Once again a festivity forms the background to these musical 'stories' – *Egmont Stories, Family Scenes with Fathers, Wedding* (Bw90). This is clear both from the superscriptions, such as *Suitable tempo for a ball*, or *Fast and Festive*, and in the various dance rhythms. *The Voice from the Distance* in the last *Novellette* reveals his thoughts about his 'distant beloved' (for Hatem in the *Der west-östliche Divan*, Suleika is also the 'symbol of the distance'[53]), while the two quotations from Beethoven's cycle *To the Distant Beloved* refer to her as well. The cycle opens with a festive march, there is a wild gigue in the *Intermezzo* of the third piece, followed by a waltz, a polonaise, a gavotte with *great humour*, and a prestissimo minuet, like the one Beethoven wrote for his Fourth Symphony, while another fast minuet forms the conclusion. It can be seen from the movement indicated in all of these that the dance is a musical metaphor for society. Within this festive setting the voice of one particular person can be heard: turbulent passages are followed again and again by reflective sections like monologues, by lyrical songs, references and quotations; sudden harmonic changes, hesitations and fermatas indicate irritation within the background of the dance. This glittering festive world sometimes becomes a labyrinth where the individual loses his way and his point of reference, so that general vitality, the 'joy of being alive' can turn sinister and can only be perceived occasionally. This can be seen in hesitations, in sections *becoming faster and faster* (No 6), and in headlong fugato passages (No 5),[54] in strange syncopations and semitone intervals (No 3), and in the uneven rhythm of the waltz. The last *Novellette*, unlike the others, opens with a passionate Florestan type of song. In answer there are three quotations from Clara's *Notturno* Op 6 No 2, the *Voice from the Distance*, at first very softly, simultaneously with the music of the hunting trio, but as if from a completely different place. The reference is clearer in the repeat, and finally, before the festive conclusion, the quotation is *forte,* with strong accents, as if the isolation of the individual had been broken – like Schumann's dreams for the future, of which he wrote to Clara in April 1838: *It will be a life of poetry and flowers – we will play together like the angels, and compose and bring joy to mankind* (Bw127).

Schumann had been looking for an opportunity since September 1838 to publish his journal in Vienna in order to give it greater scope and hence to induce Wieck to come round. In the belief that *the happiness of his whole life* (NF135) was dependent on this undertaking in Vienna, he had embarked on *a journey to his new future* (Bw217) and was even planning to settle in the city permanently, hoping that he would be offered a professorship at the Vienna conservatory. He was aware that censorship under Metternich was severe. He also knew that *no foreigner* had been *permitted* to produce a journal (Bw259), but it was only when some of his books – Jean Paul and Byron – had been confiscated that he really understood that the censors could *destroy everything* (Bw273). All his careful planning, his numerous letters and contacts during the six months of his stay, his dreams of a *new home* (Bw252), came to nothing, shattered by the fears of publishers over censorship problems. Despite making many new acquaintances – with Franz Xaver Mozart, Sigismund Thalberg, Ole Bull – and despite many interesting encounters, such as those with Grillparzer or Lenau, Schumann had no close friends in Vienna. He was *very lonely* (T2,80), as can be seen from the despondent monologue of the *Romanze* from Op 26, a reminiscence on Clara's *Andantino*. The meeting with Mozart's son, rather like the one he had had with Goethe's grandson, confirmed him in the belief that they were all *thoroughly brave Epigones* (T2,74). Schumann had sought to create *something poetic, lively and open-minded* in Vienna (Bw286), but returned to Leipzig at the beginning of April, thoroughly downcast. Meanwhile, in January 1839, he had discovered a large number of posthumous manuscripts by Franz Schubert in the house of his brother Ferdinand: *several operas, four great masses, four or five symphonies and much else besides* (NF425). Schumann busied himself preparing them for publication, and immediately sent the Symphony in C major, *the greatest piece of instrumental music to have been written since Beethoven* (NF175), to Mendelssohn, who performed it in March.

During his time in Vienna Schumann had been writing for the piano, including the melancholy *Humoreske*, Op 20, and the *Nachtstücke*, Op 23, (originally entitled *Leichenphantasie*, Corpse

Fantasy), and also four movements of his Op 26, portraying the experience of his months in Vienna, and including an ironic answer for the Viennese censors. The title, *Faschingsschwank aus Wien* (Carnival Pranks from Vienna) hides a *great romantic sonata* (NF150) that opens with a rondo, usually to be found as a sonata's finale, and closes with a movement in sonata form. The mask of harmlessness is deceptive: the subject of *Faschingsschwank* is civic emancipation. In the first movement the opening motif heralds the revolutionary mood, as do the repeated fanfares of force and the unmistakable quotation from the *Marseillaise*, banned in Vienna; after the reference to the revolutionary hymn, played fortissimo in bright A flat major and only lightly concealed in triple time, the call to fight is intensified until the turbulent finale [of this movement], opening with a fanfare, becomes a direct expression of belligerence. Hope for a new *poetic epoch* is expressed in the

Intermezzo (which was written later), a nocturne-like movement, though to be played at a faster speed with greater energy. Its passionate tone, harmonic and tonal vagueness, and its speech-like melody characterised by suspensions, that move over a blurred and restless background of sound, evoke a distant future when man will return home, as can be heard in the deep E flat major of its conclusion.

Clara Wieck. Lithograph by F Giere

In February 1839 Clara Wieck set off on a concert tour to Paris, this time without her father, who had not only refused his support, but also compelled her to engage a Frenchwoman as her companion in place of her trusted maid Nanni. Schumann was amazed how she survived eight months abroad, dependent entirely on herself, despite so many difficulties, and despite the revolutionary unrest in May, especially as she was subjected to greater animosity than ever from her father. When Schumann applied to the Leipzig court on 15 July 1839, to force Wieck's agreement to his marriage, he was initiating a debilitating legal case that lasted for more than a year. Wieck refused to attend the 'reconciliation sessions' ordered by the court, so Clara had to travel in vain each time from Berlin, where she was living with her mother. Instead, Wieck drafted a comprehensive document in which he set out numerous accusations and defamatory charges against Schumann, which he laid before the court yet again on 18 December: he accused Schumann of being 'lazy and unreliable' and alleged that he hardly paid any attention to his journal, that he was bound to 'fold' sooner or later and that he was completely unable to support himself. Schumann's lack of success with his

First journey of a steam-engine from Alten to Leipzig on 24 April 1837

'diffuse piano compositions, almost unplayable' betrayed his lack of 'solid study'. In addition, he was 'childish, unmanly' and 'completely unsuited to social life' on account of his 'gauche behaviour'; he had promised marriage to Ernestine von Fricken, and was only interested in Clara Wieck because of the 'earnings' he could make from her concerts. And also, 'Schumann had a tendency to drink'.[55] Wieck had this document lithographed and distributed to his acquaintances, even those in other cities. Although Schumann's friends David, Mendelssohn, Verhulst and Friese stood by him, the accusations were humiliating. He had made enquiries in 1838 about the possibility of a doctorate from Leipzig University. Now he requested Dr Keferstein, who occasionally wrote for Schumann's journal under the pseudonym of K Stein and who lived in Jena, if he would make application on his behalf, since he could produce this before the court in his defence. Three weeks later the Faculty of Philosophy at the University of Jena did in fact confer an honorary doctorate on the composer, critic and editor Robert Schumann, in recognition of his achievements.

The legal case had been such a drain on Schumann's nerves that he was hardly able to do any work before the summer of 1839. In early August he suffered the first of his acoustic hallucinations, hearing in his head *constant painful and tormenting music* (T2,61). This afflicted him again in November. In addition there were worries about the Schumann publishing business after the death of his oldest brother on 6 April 1839. Towards the end of the year Schumann was suffering from such a *longing for death, and black melancholy* that he *shut himself up for days on end* (Bw304).

The court decided in the middle of January 1840 to pursue only the accusation of alcoholism. Both sides had to produce evidence within fourteen days. In his 'refutation document' of 13 February, Schumann set out his financial position in detail – his total assets were 12,688 Reichstaler with an annual guaranteed income of 1,500 Reichstaler; the journal had 443 subscribers and produced an annual net income for its publisher, Friese, of 1,500 Reichstaler. Schumann refuted Wieck's accusations with documents of honorary memberships, with evidence of his doctorate, and with references from prominent colleagues on his compositions. He countered the charge of alcoholism with the accusation that Wieck himself regularly took part in evening gatherings at wine houses. As Wieck could produce no witnesses to give evidence on his behalf, the court finally consented, on 1 August 1840, to the marriage of Robert Schumann and Clara Wieck. They were married on 12 September in Schönefeld, near Leipzig.

Songs, Symphonies and Quartets

Suddenly at the beginning of 1840 Schumann started to compose only songs, *I have written about 27 pages since yesterday*, he wrote to Clara in February. *Oh Clara, what bliss it is to write songs; I have missed that for so long* (Jb309). Before that time he had not considered *song composition to be a great art* (NF158), and had usually left the reviewing of vocal music to his colleague Lorenz. The speed with which the songs were composed – by the end of the year there were 138 – sometimes seemed *quite uncanny* even to him (Jb314). He set poems by his contemporaries, Heine, Rückert, Eichendorff, Geibel, Hebbel, Chamisso, Kerner and Andersen, and made song cycles as Beethoven and Schubert had done, mostly to texts by one single poet. Schumann had noted that the accompaniments for Schubert's songs were *often too copious*, (GS1,270) and his generation had learned *to maintain one rhythm, one accompanying figure from the beginning to the end* (GS2,336). Gradually composers were developing *a more artistic and deeper expressiveness in song to reflect the new spirit of poetry* (GS2,147), and this could be seen in the works of Norbert Burgmüller or Robert Franz. Since *the piano* had begun to seem *too narrow* to him, Schumann himself was leading the *avant garde* (NF153) of song composers. Apart from the cycles, Schumann was also writing single songs, romances, ballades, duets, choral movements, and working with vernacular music, as well as devotional and *domestic music* (GS1,298). There were songs of knights and Minnesingers, from a strangely idealising historical perspective, for example, *Blondels Lied* (Blondel's Song, Op 53, No 1), *Der Page* (The Page, Op 30, No 2) or *Der Hidalgo* (The Hidalgo, Op 30, No 3). Schumann's wedding present to his wife was a volume of 26 songs to texts by various poets, bound in red velvet, with the title *Myrthen* (Myrtles, Op 25) though these do not really form a cycle. The third song, *Der Nussbaum* (The Walnut Tree) is an example of the new, close unity between piano and voice. The vocal line becomes one of the voices woven into the structure of the piano accompaniment, carrying the melody forward. There is a melodic figure running throughout this song like a leitmotif, a sort of promise, (similar to the wish figure in the first of the *Kinderszenen*) singing of *next year's* happiness – a constant subject in Schumann's letters.

A note Schumann made in March 1833 runs: *musical poems underlaid with songs by H Heine* (T1,417); seven years later poems from Heine's *Buch der Lieder* (Book of Songs) would form the basis for two cycles (Op 24 and Op 48). The inner unity of the *Liederkreis* (Cycle of Songs) Op 24, setting nine Heine poems, is apparent not only in the pattern of keys, but in the epilogue of the last song, referring back to the final bar of the first. Schumann's cycle about the loneliness and impatience of the waiting lover, estranged from his beloved, the misery of being abandoned, is not only based on personal experience, but reflects the spirit of his age. The individual's isolation and fear are expressed in the image of the *glittering* Rhine, whose depths mask *death and darkness* (No 7), to be seen also in the unaccompanied ending of the fourth song, where the first person narrator is almost struck dumb by fear. He looks back at images of lost beauty, as in the song *Schöne Wiege meiner Leiden* (Fair Cradle of my Sorrows), with an epilogue reminiscent of *Mondnacht* (Moonlight), or in the third song where *old dreams* are heard in the speechless voice of the instrument.

Schumann met Franz Liszt for the first time in March 1840, and the visit *disconcerted him completely* (NF187). He was fascinated by this pianist, who played in such an *extraordinary* manner, *daring and bold, then gently and poetically* in a way he had *never heard* before (Jb310). He published two long articles in the *Neue Zeitschrift* on Liszt's concerts in Dresden and Leipzig, where he considered that Liszt could only be compared with Paganini. At the last concert Liszt had performed several pieces from *Carnaval*, but Schumann reported *that however brilliantly he played them the majority of the audience had not been moved* (GS1,484). Schumann was more critical of Liszt as a composer: *His world* is no longer mine, he wrote to Clara, *there is something tawdry about it* (Jb310).

The *Liederkreis*, Op 39, was composed in May [1840]. Schumann had put together texts from various collections of Eichendorff's poems.[56] There is no 'story' to unite them as there had been in the *Liederkreis*, Op 24 – instead Schumann used recurring motifs, of distance, deception, night, loneliness, home, to express the experience how the individual feels like a stranger in his time, with all hope pinned on a distant future. The twelve songs are unified by an arch-like arrangement of keys, that spans from F sharp minor to F sharp major, and by common structures. The interval of the fifth acts as a cipher for the circle, occurring as E-H-E (H = B natural) in Nos 3, 5, 7, and 9 (Ehe is the German word for marriage). In all the songs (except No 7), there is a sequence of falling intervals derived from the chord of the seventh; it is only finally in *Frühlingsnacht* (Spring Night), where the *wonder* has become reality, that the motif of the broken chord of the seventh is allowed to

Franz Liszt. Lithograph by Joseph Kriehuber, c. 1830

rise; in *Mondnacht* it is augmented by the ninth, spanning four octaves at the beginning of the song, like a bridge arching between earth and heaven. The dream of future happiness is embodied in the sixth song *Schöne Fremde* with its fluid tonality (D flat minor – C sharp minor – B major); in the song *Wehmut* (Sadness), where *longing* reveals a completely new realm with the sudden move from E to D major; in *Mondnacht* where time seems to stand still, suggested by repeated notes, and where 'home' appears in this unreal world as the single destination for which the poet longs.[57] Right at the beginning of the cycle, the first song speaks of the isolation of the first person narrator in the world; fear is expressed in the sudden change from F sharp minor to the Neapolitan G major: *And no one remembers me here*. Unusual harmonies indicate the motif of aimless wandering and disillusion: in *Waldesgespräch* (Overheard in the Woods) modulations moving aimlessly *back and forth* accompany the meanderings of the hunting horn; each time an imperfect cadence indicates that the wanderer cannot bring the *beautiful bride* home, and at the end he realises he has been deceived. Even the *peaceful* calm of nature and the *lively* game of the musicians in the song *Auf einer Burg* (On a Castle) are deceptive; some unnamed misfortune is indicated by the juxtaposition of a chorale with astonishingly modern-sounding dissonances, and harmonies that have no aim. The image of the wedding is set in the same oppressive way as that of the knight turning to stone, expressing a feeling of paralysis that is typical of the perception of time during the Restoration. *Everything is now standing so dreadfully still*, Schumann wrote in the summer of 1838 (Bw182). The song *Zwielicht*[58] (Twilight) speaks of the treacherous peace. Schumann quoted this in 1849, as revolution had finally put an abrupt end to peace, in the manuscript of the seventh *Waldszene*, Op 82, *Vogel als Prophet: Beware! Be cheerful and vigilant!*

Schumann wrote *Dichterliebe* (A Poet's Love), a new cycle using 16 poems[59] from Heine's *Buch der Liebe*, at almost the same time as the *Liederkreis*, Op 39. The subject of these poems is a great love, from its beginning to its end. *Im wunderschönen Monat Mai* (In the lovely month of May), which opens the sequence, contains the essence of magic as love unfolds: the arching melodic line resembles a promise of what might be, as if there were a hidden melody, from the fifth to the ninth to the seventh. Dominant harmonies are so strong here that even the final bars do not return to the home key of F sharp minor. The divergence between dream and reality becomes ever clearer (Nos 13, 14, 15), pain lurks behind a mask of irony (Nos 11, 16), loss of identity is expressed in the metaphor of the broken heart (Nos 7, 8, 11) – in the eighth song the words *my heart broke in two* are set against a break in the musical line. In the ninth song *Das ist ein Flöten und Geigen* (There's a blowing of flutes and a scraping of fiddles), a dance scene becomes an image for the isolation of the individual, as similarly in the ballads *Der arme Peter* (Poor Peter), Op 53 No 3 and *Der Spielman* (The Minstrel), Op 40 No 4. In the postlude, when the rotating figure in the piano accompaniment returns, with its senseless mechanical repetitions (an idea later adopted by Gustav Mahler), the wedding dance and the dance of death become one. The expressive E flat minor song *Ich hab' im Traum geweinet* (I wept in my dream) is similar to the *quasi parlando* Schumann used in his piano music; the unaccompanied vocal line is interrupted here by lurching bars of the piano – the extremely sharp tension between the dissonant chords and the voice at *Ich wachte auf* (I awoke) in the third verse is a device that was later used by the Expressionists. The cyclical character of *Dichterliebe* (Poet's Love) is emphasised in the postlude to the last song; in place of the expected final chord in C sharp minor, there follows a long epilogue in D flat major, expressing what the words of the final verse *Liebe und Schmerz* (Love and Pain) cannot say, and serving as a commentary on the whole cycle.

The Chamisso song cycle, *Frauenliebe und-leben*, Op 42, has particular biographical significance; Schumann had his own visions for the ring motif of the fourth song and the wedding march in the postlude of the fifth. The music of this cycle often contradicts the eloquent perfect happiness of the text, both in its tempo and its passion. The image conjured up by the words is of a woman content to merely be the humble servant of her lord and master: the lines in the fifth song, for instance, *Let me bow to my lord in all reverence and humility*, are set musically against the sense of the words. In the epilogue at the end of the cycle the sarabande rhythm, taken from the opening love song, suggests the proximity of love and death, as the piano reminisces on *lost happiness*.

Schumann believed that his songs would appeal to audiences more than his piano music, but the song cycles, with their careful sequence of tonalities, were not suited to concerts with mixed programmes. Instead it was the *Rheinlied* which had a great success at the end of the year. This was a song composed with choral societies and music festivals in mind, easy for amateurs to sing. There was a competition, in December 1840, for the best setting of the patriotic poem *Der deutsche Rhein* by Nicolaus Becker, proof of the popular longing at this time for a German Reich. Schumann's *Rheinlied* did not win the competition, but within a month 1,500 copies had been sold, and it had even been turned into a *galoppade* (T2,127). *They shall not take it/ the free German Rhine*: how hollow the patriotic sentiments have been, is expressed with an hypocritical and pathetic idea of freedom that could hardly hide imperialistic claims, for which *the last man's bones be sacrificed*. The form of this song was aesthetically unsatisfactory, as can be seen in the mismatch between the forces required (solo voice, choir and piano) with the musical content. Schumann used more economical forces to set Heine's ballad *Die beiden Grenadiere* (The two Grenadiers, Op 49 No 1), which portrays the soldiers marching in step – their worries about wife and child overlaid by the jaunty marching rhythm. They can only give proper expression to their feelings as they imagine a burial with full military honours – the accompanying triplets reveal their sentimentality. The irony in the music is particularly evident in the comic antithesis of the last verses, with the image of the sentinel lying *quietly* in his grave, listening, while the wish to *guard the Emperor* is set against the Marseillaise, the Hymn of the Revolution. At the end the sadly ironic postlude mourns only

Clara and Robert Schumann. Lithograph by Eduard Kaiser, 1847

the victims, expressed by an alienation of the second part of the melodic line and a cliché-ridden military accompaniment (bar 2) that resolve into sort of requiem.

In September 1840 Robert Schumann gave his wife an album for her birthday. This was to be a *diary of their marriage*, and in it they were to record their thoughts on *household and marriage*, on their own compositions and those of other artists, but also comments and requests *where a word alone is not enough*. Clara had signed a set of statutes, as a 'devoted wife' (T2,99), one of which was that they would each make entries in the diary, on alternate weeks. Robert had written of the *greatest happiness* (T2,100). Was this the happiness she had meant when she said it would be 'almost too much to bear?' (Bw593) Clara, too, called this time her 'happiest three months' though in reality she was constantly sad, regularly felt 'exhausted and tired' and often had to lie down. Although there were two pianos in the apartment, she was only permitted to play when her husband was not at home, owing to the 'thin walls' (T2,130,117, 144), so she soon felt she was 'going backwards'. She had to turn down offers of concerts: 'Robert does not wish it', she wrote in the diary (T2,110,103). The pianist Amalie Rieffel was a 'dangerous rival', as was also Camilla Pleyel, who had recently been taken up by Wieck, and Robena Laidlaw to whom Robert Schumann had dedicated his *Fantasiestücke*, Op 12. In February 1841 when Thalberg gave a concert in Leipzig Clara was more afraid than ever that she would no longer be able to keep pace with the competition. She was unwilling to give up the concert tours to Holland and Russia, was unhappy at the prospect of 'sitting still all winter', and was sensitive to any criticism from her husband. Clara was continually fearful that she would not live up to his expectations, since she believed that she had no 'personality' and was convinced that she would soon be forgotten by the outside world. She was not permitted to 'disturb' her husband when he was composing, so she mostly conducted a 'written conversation' with him, and since she could not 'catch hold' of him, she at least could write of intimacies in the diary (T2,121,125,121, 111,121).

They had many visitors in the Inselstrasse; artists like Ole Bull, Livia Frege, Amalie Rieffel, Sophie Schloss, Zuccalmaglio, Thalberg, Marschner, Henselt from St Petersburg, William Sterndale Bennett from London, Verhulst, the conductor of the Euterpe music society's concerts. Wilhelmine Schröder-Devrient, the famous soprano at the Dresden court theatre, whom Schumann had so much admired in Fidelio in Leipzig, visited, as well as Pauline Viardot – to Clara Schumann the 'dearest and most gifted of all artists' (T2,267) – and then of course David and Mendelssohn, later also Gade, who had become the second conductor at the

The house in which Clara and Robert Schumann lived in the Inselstrasse, Leipzig

Gewandhaus in 1843, Hiller, Spohr, Berlioz, Robert Franz and Wagner. If the guests stayed to dinner, Clara had 'housewifely concerns' (T2,103). Sometimes they sang Schumann's songs, and if David and Mendelssohn were amongst the guests, they would play trios or quartets. But Schumann complained: *May heaven forgive me, but I cannot listen to so much music* (T2,102). Robert and Clara were themselves frequent guests of the List family – Clara had been friends with the daughters of the political economist for many years, of the industrialist Harkort *where things were very superior* (T2,151), of the Mendelssohns, the Davids, the publishers Härtel, Kistner, Hofmeister and Brockhaus, and of old friends such as Friese, Becker and Reuter. Moscheles came for a visit from England in October, and Clara was afraid of playing to him as her 'fingers were stiff' from 'sewing and writing' (T2,134), but she did perform a few pieces from *Kreisleriana* and was persuaded to play Bach's Triple Concerto in D minor with Moscheles and Mendelssohn at a soirée at the Gewandhaus. Schumann did have some feeling for her difficult position, and resolved to do something about it *later* on, so that she could practise as much as she needed (T2,132). Together they studied Bach's *Well-Tempered Clavier,* and then Beethoven's sonatas the next year, followed by the scores of Beethoven's symphonies. Schumann taught her how to write fugues and encouraged her to read – Jean Paul, Shakespeare, Goethe, but also Victor Hugo, though she abhorred his *Notre Dame de Paris*, considering it 'flippant' and 'unrealistic' (T2,150), and Robert was continually asking her to compose. However, Clara herself thought that she 'had no talent as a composer' (T2,141) and instead made *fair copies* of his songs, *a bitter work* (T2,107), and gave piano lessons for no fee, which she found most unseemly at first. And so she practised modesty. At Christmas-time she presented her husband with three songs: 'just a rather weak attempt, with no real worth'. To Robert, on the other hand, she seemed to be *a much clearer musician than before* (T2,134).

Clara's style as a composer and her musical judgement had in fact changed. In 1839 she had still been saying: 'Listen, Robert, won't you write another piece that is brilliant and easily understood — something without any superscript', 'not too long and not too short?' (L1,311) Whereas previously she had regarded Spohr, to whom she had dedicated her piano concerto, as her authority on matters of style, she had adored Bellini's music, and had preferred to play virtuoso pieces by fashionable composers in her concerts, now she shared Robert's enthusiasm for Bach, and played Beethoven's sonatas in public concerts, as did Mendelssohn, making a strict distinction between 'true music' and the 'virtuoso'. In fact bravura pieces by 'Henselt, Thalberg, and Liszt etc.' had become 'quite repugnant' to her (T2,181). Critical opinion had placed her with the 'Romantic School' on the strength of her piano pieces, Op 5 and Op 6, in the style of Chopin. The growing influence of Schumann was clear in her Three Romances, Op 11, written in Paris in 1839, especially in the polyphonic voice-leading of the Romance in G minor. Schumann had also provided the theme for her three fugues, Op 16. Her earlier writing, Op 7 to Op 10, had consisted of virtuoso compositions, designed to cause a 'furore' (Bw469) at her own concerts, whereas the Romances, Op 11, the four movement Sonata in G minor, the *Pièces fugitives*, Op 15, and the Three Preludes and Fugues, Op 16, were considered works in the new Romantic idiom. Robert wrote to her on the subject of the G minor Romance: *You make me complete as a composer, as I complete you* (Bw629).

Robert Schumann's influence can be seen even more clearly in her songs than in her pieces for piano, since she chose her texts on his advice. *Am Strande* (On the Shore) to a text by Robert Burns, is reminiscent of *In der Nacht* (In the Night) from Schumann's *Fantasiestücke* Op 12. The motif of water separating lovers echoes Robert's commentary on this fantasy, which referred to the story of Hero and Leander. Elements from Schumann's songs can be found in the lively harmony, the sustained rhythms of the accompaniment, the individual motifs for the piano and the declamatory style of the song. *Auf einer Burg* from the Eichendorff cycle, with its old-fashioned harmonic style, seems to have been the model for Clara's *Volkslied* (Folksong), a setting of a poem by Heine, where the eloquence of the epilogue is reminiscent of those by her husband. Shortly after Christmas Robert conceived the idea of producing, jointly with Clara, a book of songs setting Rückert's *Liebesfrühling* (Love's springtime). He kept nagging her to write music for a few of the texts until, by the time of his birthday in June 1841 she had written four songs. These included *Er ist gekommen* (He has come), whose theme tune recurs in her *Scherzo* Op 14 and in the sonata. Schumann published three of her songs alongside nine of his own as a joint work by *Robert and Clara Schumann.*[60] The style of this cycle was so uniform that critics were hard pressed to decide which of them had composed the individual songs.

Clara's song *Why do you want to ask others* was published by Schumann in his song cycle *Liebesfrühling* op. 37

There were many opportunities to listen to music in Leipzig, particularly during the winter season. These included the subscription concerts in the Gewandhaus conducted by Mendelssohn, his 'historical concerts' of choral music, particularly Bach and Handel – at Easter 1841 the *St Matthew Passion* was performed in St Thomas's Church for the first time since Bach's death; there were 12 concerts given by the Euterpe music society at the Hôtel de Pologne, and chamber music evenings in the Gewandhaus – the so-called 'musical evening entertainments'; then there were benefit concerts, and concerts put on by visiting virtuosos, and organ recitals, with for instance Mendelssohn as soloist – the proceeds from these funded the construction of the Bach Memorial, dedicated in 1843. There were soirées in private houses as well. Clara and Robert also went to the opera from time to time, or to plays in the new theatre. In springtime and in summer they would walk out as far as Connewitz, Gohlis or Knauthain. They took their first holiday together, travelling by steam train to Dresden then on into 'Saxon Switzerland', then in August 1842 they visited Carlsbad and Marienbad.

Robert Schumann's artistic productivity between 1840 and 1844 clearly indicate how much the discovery of Schubert's great C major Symphony had meant for him. In October of 1840 – his 'song year' – Schumann himself was working on a symphony in C minor which would not *come out right* (T2,112). He had long wanted to write *a piano concerto and a symphony* (T2,122), but was apprehensive of attempting anything symphonic after Beethoven, while his bitter experience with his G minor symphony had persuaded him to work in other genres for the time being. He had *symphonic scruples* at a later date, too, (T3,174), thinking that Beethoven's Ninth had *exhausted* the field and there were only *echoes of what had gone before* to be heard *everywhere around* (GS1,70, 312). In a long article in 1835 Schumann had praised Berlioz' *Symphonie fantastique* as being progressive – he took the opposite opinion from Fétis on its 'barbaric style' (GS2,379). Schumann was interested in its close analogy with drama, with *free speech* (GS1,74), but this path, with its *eccentricity* and its rough-hewn programme writing (GS1,85,83), was not for him. The *absolute independence* from his idol Beethoven that he could see in Schubert's symphony, discovered amongst his posthumous manuscripts, was the trigger: to Schumann this music seemed to resemble a work of literature with its 'speaking' instrumental voices – it was a fascinating example of a modern symphony (GS1,463).

The particella of Schumann's Symphony in B flat major, Op 38, was completed in just four days, from 23 to 26 January 1841. The instrumentation was written 'in a storm' (T2,145), and the *Spring Symphony* was ready on 20 February (NF 204). The opening of the work is reminiscent of Schubert's Symphony in C major. The movements originally had titles – *The Beginning of Spring*, *Evening*, *Merry Playmates*, *Spring in Full Bloom* (L2,27). It was inspired by a poem by Adolf Böttger, who translated Byron and who would later work on the text of *Das Paradies und die Peri* (Paradise and the Peri). The last lines of this poem ran: *O wende, wende Deinen Lauf/Im Thale blüht der Frühling auf!* (O turn, turn from your course/In the valley spring is blossoming) (JD 245). The symphonic motto of the opening picks up not only the rhythm of the words, but also the imperative they contain. It was to sound *as if from on high*, or *as a call to awaken*, wrote Schumann (E1,293). Indeed with the natural trumpets and horns of the day it would have sounded much sharper in performance than now. The poem seeks to dispel an unvoiced threat through a new beginning. Likewise, the opening movement of the symphony seems to contain traces of terrors from the past: this can be seen in the painful motif of the wind instruments in bar 5, in the minor tonalities, in the development theme, as well as in the references to *Kreisleriana*. This is contrasted by a determination for a new beginning: with the rhythmical dominance of the motto that marks the principal theme, the second subject and the final group,[61] in the continuously soaring figures, the trumpet calls and the sforzato accents. The climax is reached when, at the beginning of the recapitulation, the theme returns as a triple forte, now harmonised and extended over seven bars. It is only in the following coda, bars 438 ff, that the strings play a theme marked *dolce*, apparently the delayed second subject, in reality the rhythm of the main theme, lightly disguised. Contrast in the first movement is not so much created between two themes as between past and future. On the one hand the influence of Beethoven's Symphony in B flat major can be clearly seen in the general layout and in various details; on the other hand, the gradual development of the final theme – from rhythmic outline to its complete form at the close of the recapitulation (bars 237–261) – points forward to the thematic apotheosis of the late Romantics. The idea of a symphony where the concluding movement would complete the opening, can be seen in the anticipation of the scherzo's theme into the *Larghetto* (bars 113 ff), and in the unresolved ending of the *Scherzo*, as well as in the interweaving that occurs throughout the work that requires the listener to hear 'ahead and back', as necessitated by Jean Paul's flute-player Vult in his musical 'syntax'.[62] References are created through rhythmic variations, through the impression of rising trumpet calls, turns, and cadences for solo flute. The additive procedure shows an affinity with the literary novel, while the self-quotations from *Kreisleriana* are reminiscent of Jean Paul.[63] Another comparison with the literary novel can be made in the integration of what could be regarded as foreign elements: the second movement becomes a song with varied verse structures, the Scherzo with its two trios has a five-section form with a change of time, as does the second piece of *Kreisleriana*.

Mendelssohn conducted the first performance of the symphony on 31 March at the Gewandhaus. Clara played at the same concert – the first time she had appeared for a long time. The critical reviews in the *Allgemeine Musikalische Zeitung* and in the *Leipziger Zeitung* were somewhat restrained, but Schumann himself was pleased at his success (T2,157) and especially at Mendelssohn's praise. Clara, who had not thought her husband 'capable' of writing a symphony, felt 'awe-struck' at his achievement (T2,143). Further performances of the Spring Symphony followed in Weimar, Bremen, Hamburg, Berlin, The Hague and Rotterdam, thus making the composer known beyond Leipzig.

Schumann had been making sketches for piano concertos ever since his years in Zwickau. He had no desire to write a work in the style of virtuoso concertos of the past, so he had to *think of something else*. The formal boundaries of the genres *between symphony, concerto and grand sonata* had been overcome in 1839, in the *Konzertsatz* in D minor (Bw 367). In May 1841 he wrote, in the space of two weeks, a *Phantasie* in A minor for piano and orchestra in which he again combined the styles of symphonic and chamber music, while compressing the three movements into a single one. This differed from the G minor Concerto, Op 25 by Mendelssohn, often played by Clara, or Spohr's Violin Concerto Op 47, 'a vocal scene', where the three movements followed each other without pause and were linked by recurring themes. Schumann's *Phantasie* combined sonata form and cyclical concerto form, although the traditional sequence of movements for the latter – a slow movement between two fast ones with an introduction – was still apparent. His, however, also contained elements of a sonata. It is based on one single theme, introduced elegiacally by the oboe. All the other themes are derived from this: the C major variation as a cheerful auxiliary theme, the fanfare of the climax in bars 134 ff, the A flat major melody in 6/4 time that seems to be moving to a higher sphere, and finally the swift march in the coda. Seemingly new figures grow out of the individual elements of the theme, such as the introductory cascade from the third that characterises the beginning of the theme. The monothematic nature of this music reflects the multiple forms of self presented by Schumann elsewhere, as the figures of Florestan and Eusebius in the *Davidsbündlertänzen*. The sound of the music itself also reinforces the impression of a spoken monologue. Clara commented that the piano 'is most skilfully interwoven with the orchestra' (T2,180) so that the orchestral colours appear to augment the piano, to create just one single body of sound. Schumann could not find a publisher for his Phantasie, so in 1845 he added two further movements to make the Piano Concerto, Op 54. These two linked additions were an Intermezzo in F major, resembling chamber music, and, to balance the elegiac nature of the Phantasie's theme, an A major finale, with a particularly dance-like character, alternating between 3/2 and 3/4 time (as for example in the writing for piano and orchestra in bars 231 ff). A motif with a triple upbeat links all three movements, with back references, such as the sudden quotation of the beginning of the Phantasie theme at the end of the Intermezzo, or the falling fifths from the Intermezzo in the coda of the Finale (bars 24 and 860 ff). The many musical quotations are repeated in the references whose hidden character corresponds to the monolodic nature of this work, all point to Clara: to her own piano concerto, Op 7, also in A minor with a Romanze in A Flat major on whose theme Robert Schumann based his concerto, and to whose scoring (for cello and piano) the central section of the Intermezzo refers; the Phantasie theme itself echoes Clara Wieck's *Notturno*, Op 6 No 2, quoted in Robert Schumann's eighth *Novellette* as the *Stimme aus der Ferne* (Voice from the Distance); and finally there are references to Florestan's aria *In des Lebens Frühlingstagen* (In the springtime of life) from *Fidelio* (Act 2, 11), that in itself can be taken as a reference to Clara.

| 1. Satz | C | H | A | A |

Piano Concerto Op. 54

At the end of May, immediately after he had finished his Phantasie, Schumann had a *sudden burst of inspiration* (T3,184) to write a 'new single-movement symphony' (T2,169). The first draft of this was complete three months later. From the very introduction, the vision of this work is clearly beyond here and now — in the vagueness in tonality and time, in the unrest of its circling shape and in its trumpet calls. The theme of the exposition, with its abrupt phrases denoting deep agitation, is unresolved, as are almost all the melodic figures, as if they were merely provisional, until the themes of the first movement eventually prevail in the development section. The main theme only achieves its own individual form in the finale (bars 17ff). The open conclusions of the first three movements, each without reprise, and the tonal progression within these movements (D minor–D major; D minor–A major; D minor–B flat major) emphasise the sequential nature of this composition; the fanfares and the unison fermata of the outside movements point to expectations for the future, as does the forward reference to the Romanze before the coda of the first movement. In the same way the heavy use of sequences is not to be seen as a lack of compositional inspiration, but rather the expression of the general obsession about moving forward. The four individual movements of this work, linked closely as they are through monothematic material, once again contain a wealth of references. On the manuscript of the second version Schumann called this work a *Symphonistische Phantasie*; this new aesthetic form reflects the feelings of his generation, whose thoughts were firmly fixed on the future, and who regarded their own period as merely transitional. Dissatisfaction and unease with the present can be seen in an intense turning to a past that is still present in recollection. This symphony contains many musical quotations and references, most frequently in the final movement. The trio of the Scherzo refers back to the Romanze, itself firmly rooted in the past – not only in its title, but also in the lament for oboe and cellos over a pizzicato accompaniment that sounds like chords played by a guitar. The archaic harmony of the music (originally scored for guitar) points to a distance in space and time.

The Symphony in D minor was first performed on 6 December 1841, at the same time as the *Ouvertüre*, Op 52. The real sensation at this concert, however, was the *Hexameron*, a set of variations by six different virtuosos on a duet by Bellini which was played on two pianos by Liszt and Clara Schumann, and described in the diary as 'an absolutely brilliant piece' (T2,195). Schumann set his symphony aside for ten years before revising it. In March 1853 it was performed in Düsseldorf as his Fourth Symphony in D minor, Op 120. Schumann continued to work on symphonic projects throughout 1841, despite periods of exhaustion recurring with ever greater frequency. By the autumn he was at work on a *little symphony in C minor* (T2,187).

1841 had been a year of considerable upheaval, with the various performances of the *Spring Symphony* in the Gewandhaus, in the Euterpe, and then in Weimar, with Liszt's visit in December, as exhausting as usual, and with the birth of the Schumanns' daughter, Marie, on 1 September. Both parents were delighted at this event, but their financial worries now increased, since Schumann's fees for his compositions and his income from his journalistic work were insufficient for a growing family. He was obliged to sell securities, and diminish his capital. His financial sorrows were such that at the end of the year he was obliged to borrow fifty talers from Carl Voigt (T3,202). For a time he believed that an American tour – *a terrible decision* – would bring in so much all at once that they would be secure *for the whole of their lives* (T2,206). Clara, who at this time often felt discontented and irritated with her situation, would have liked nothing better than to perform in concerts and thus to improve their financial situation. Was she to leave her talents quite unused on his account? But was he to *put aside his talents* in order to act *as her companion on tour?* (T2,206) He had been feeling *ill and melancholy* for weeks (T3,206f), but nevertheless they set off in February 1842 for a short concert tour to Bremen and Hamburg, where there was an opportunity to perform Schumann's First Symphony. In Oldenburg Clara received an invitation to court, while Robert, who had been ignored, suffered from his *lowly status*; he was also disgruntled over the *tactless review* of his symphony in a Hamburg weekly paper (T2,209,204). On 10 March he returned alone to Leipzig while his wife, with a female companion, continued on to Copenhagen – a decision made in Hamburg *after long heart-searching*. What would *the world say?* (T2,211,206) Robert Schumann went through a period of deep melancholy, at home alone with just his child and the domestic help. There were all sorts of rumours – that debts and lack of success had led to the separation from his wife; that he had left her ill in Hamburg. Wieck even spread the rumour that they were divorced. *So composing . . . was quite out of the question* (T2,219). Schumann began to drink once again, to gamble and to curse his *worthless life* (T3, 312). The separation was difficult for Clara too. She was ill in Hamburg, then a storm delayed her crossing to Copenhagen for a week, so it was two weeks before she had news of her husband and child. Nevertheless, her four weeks in Copenhagen were pleasant, and extremely successful: her 'gross takings' were 1,155 talers, of which 500 talers remained after the deduction of costs (T2,227). Schumann came to meet her *like a bridegroom, both happy and anxious. Better days are coming now*, he wrote in the diary (T2,226, 227).

They studied Haydn's and Mozart's string quartets together during the summer. Clara presented her husband with two songs for his birthday: *Sie liebten sich beide* (They loved one another) and *Liebeszauber* (Love's Magic), Op 13, Nos 2 and 3. He was hard at work on different genres of chamber works: in June and July the three String Quartets, Op 41, and in the autumn the Piano Quintet, Op 44, the Piano Quartet, Op 47, and in December the *Phantasiestücke*, Op 88, for piano, violin and cello. All three of the string quartets pay homage to Beethoven: *Nimm sie hin denn, dieser Lieder* (Take, then, these songs) is quoted in the finale of the second quartet (eg bar 37 ff), while the first movement of this quartet contains references to Beethoven's Quartet in A minor, Op 132. The adagio of the first quartet begins like that of the Ninth Symphony. Schumann, who regarded Beethoven's late quartets as *the absolute pinnacle of human art and invention* (GS1,380), worked his own Op 41 to differ from them in his use of closed forms. The principal themes are cast like three-section songs. Schumann had described Mendelssohn's Quartet in E minor, Op 44 No 2, as *very fine, clear and inspired.* (His own Op 41 is dedicated with *deep admiration* to Mendelssohn.)[64] The description might also apply to the outer movements of his own string quartets, despite his critical observation *nothing new here* (T2,46). They can be seen as 'classical' in their traditional sonata form, and in their gracefulness, closer perhaps to the works of Mozart and Haydn. The inner movements, on the other hand, whether slow or scherzo-like, reveal certain features in common with Schumann's piano music: sudden contrasts, stylised dance rhythms, lyrical monologues, reminiscences, as for example at the beginning of the reprise in the adagio of the first quartet, where the reference to Beethoven occurs three times, sounding almost tentative in the remote sequence of keys: A sharp minor – A major – F major. The four movements in a cycle are often thematically linked. The A major Quartet, Op 41 No 3, is the most intense example of the three. Here the movements are not only linked by the interval of the falling fifth, first heard in the introduction; this reappears in varying forms in the quaver section of the first movement's main theme, in the theme of the adagio and in the first couplet of the final rondo. The principal movement, where the development is reduced to a short passage in the recapitulation, is more of a character piece, despite its sonata form. This can be seen in the recitative nature of the opening, the fluttering harmonies, the various pauses, the lack of contrasts, and in the pianissimo ending to the coda, where the motif of the fifth reappears one last time, almost like a question mark in the last bar. In the set of variations, *assai agitato*, where the full theme appears for the first time in the third variation, and the exposition resembles an incomplete sketch, there is a series of stylised but unrelated dances – a gigue, a siciliano and a sarabande. The music fades into the distance, as is often the case in Schumann's dance scenes. The final rondo, however, picks up this dance-like character, its third couplet *quasi trio* being reminiscent of the gavotte in Bach's sixth French Suite. Florestan's type of humour can be seen in both movements, in the baroque disguise, the zig-zag figures of the sarabande, the surprising syncopations of the rondo-ritornell with its unexpected harmonies, and in the disturbing way Schumann plays with traditional forms: the scherzo appears as a set of variations, then as a dance suite; and in the rondo, taking two elements from the second movement, appears a *quasi trio*.

The Piano Quintet in E flat major, Op 44, is by comparison 'unclassical', in its combination of piano with string quartet, with a funeral march in place of a slow movement, with sharp contrasts and unusual tonal progressions in the finale (G minor – G major – B minor – G sharp minor – G minor – E flat major). It was composed for Clara, appearing in print for her birthday on 13 September 1843. The virtuoso piano part, which predominates throughout almost the whole work, was written with her in mind, while hidden signals, such as the falling fifth, and double fifth were references to their life together – the musical correspondence between Robert Schumann's *Impromptu*s, Op 5, and Clara Wieck's *Soirées musicales*, Op 3, and of the Sonata, Op 11, dedicated to her by *Florestan and Eusebius*. *Florestan* appears here once more in the upbeat theme of the opening, and frequently changes into his alter ego, *Eusebius* (bar 27 ff), reminders of the time when these two figures were present in Schumann's conversations with Clara Wieck. The *Eroica Symphony* is the model for the opening of the scherzo, and for the funeral march, an unusual introduction in chamber music. The funeral march lies at the heart of this work – the first movement points towards it while the scherzo and finale contain references to it – the reason for this being both the Schumanns' experiences of separation and loss. *Anfangs wollt' ich fast verzagen* – To begin with I almost wanted to give up. This chorale from the *Liederkreis*, Op 24, is quoted by Schumann in his Piano Quartet, Op 47 (First movement, bars 73 ff), written at roughly the same time. The *Allegro Brillante* of the quintet shows how difficult Schumann found it to reconcile virtuoso speed with expressiveness – at the beginning of the exposition (bars 117 ff), the relentless pathos becomes almost theatrical in its baroque sound.[65] This motif points towards the second movement, while there are numerous other references, both between the movements and as structural links to contrasting sections, demonstrating Schumann's intention to create a unity of opposites between the different movements. The finale shows most clearly the influence of Bach in the two fugal expositions integrated into a sonata rondo (bars 248 ff and 319 ff); the last of these, where the main themes of the first and fourth movements are combined into theme and counterpoint, forms the festive conclusion to the quintet.

When Adolph Henselt came to visit the Schumanns, their old plan for a concert tour to Russia was resurrected. Henselt had been living in St Petersburg for four years, earning a good living there as a pianist. Towards the end of the year Clara was overcome by 'indescribably low spirits' as she realised that her new pregnancy would prevent 'all ways of earning money' (T2,251). *Worries about the future* was one of Schumann's last entries in the diary for that year (T2,233), and in February of the following year he noted *we need more than we are earning* (T2,254). Once again he borrowed money from Voigt.

1843 was devoted to work in quite a *new genre* (E1,295), an Oratorio, not for *the prayer room*, but *for cheerful people* (NF 228). In August 1841 Emil Flechsig, his friend from student days, had brought Schumann his translation of *Lalla Rookh* by Thomas Moore. Schumann had immediately set to work on this text with the help of Adolf Böttger, and thought it was *made for music* (Boe 394). The libretto was finished in 1842, but it was not until a year later, on 23 February 1843 that Schumann began to compose the music.

The work was finished four months later. Clara, who prepared the piano score, thought it was 'the most magnificent thing he had ever written' with its 'wealth of feeling and poetry' (T2,265, 260). Schumann himself regarded *Das Paradies und die Peri* (Paradise and the Peri) as his *greatest* work hitherto (NF228), believing that *nothing like this has been done in music before* (T2,266). Moore's verse epic had appeared in 1817, two years before Goethe's *Der west-östliche Divan*, appealing to the popular taste for the exotic, as had Marschner's *Klänge aus dem Osten* (Sounds from the East) that in turn inspired Schumann to write his own oratorio. The wonders of these distant lands and times were seen as the complete antithesis of the world of the philistines. Whereas in the League of David the idea had been to break free from the Restoration into a *new poetic age* that would completely change cultural life and society with its *School of Polemics* (GS1,38, 29), this was now replaced by wishful thinking – a world that would not be changed by mankind, but would be healed through 'holy' deeds. The conflict here is between the *tyrant* and the *man of noble spirit*, seen as a figure from the Passions in a chorus of *lament* and a four part choral fugue (*Blessed is the blood/ That is shed with heroic courage for liberty*); the child praying amidst the flowers converts the hardened sinner; and the tears of the repentant sinner free Egypt from the plague. The story becomes a religious parable. The redemption scene at the end forms the climax, as it was to do later in *Faust*. The gates of heaven open for the Peri, a winged creature from Persian mythology, who, like Wagner's Kundry, bears a mysterious weight of original sin. For the Enlightenment the loss of paradise was the first step towards the emancipation of mankind, whereas Schumann's *Peri* is an allegory of the search for paradise. Wagner was also interested in 'this wonderful poem'.[66] The *Peri*, so far removed from reality, also represented a popular image of the time, often painted by the Nazarenes, of woman as the incarnation of the pure, tender and innocent, and a comparison can be made with Schumann's early devotion to the Madonna.

Schumann himself considered the way he had set parts of his composition to be progressive, and parts of the work had a song-like form. In this he was following the lead of Weber and Marschner, avoiding the traditional sequence of recitative and aria, familiar from Spohr's oratorios. The 'lyricism' of this work, the song-like character of the solo arias, choruses and narration – here divided between solo tenor, alto and mezzo-soprano narrator, vocal quartet and choir – the absence of contrasts and the use of narrative successions in place of dramatic development, can all also be seen as expressing resignation. The aggressive dynamism of the *Davidsbündler* and the *upswings* are absent in this work. Instead, the music wallows 'in unnamed joy and woe' – Nietzsche's chief criticism of Schumann's music.[67] Typical musical examples here are the

Princess Elisa Radziwill in the role of Peri
Painting by Wilhelm Hensel 1821

yearning sadness of the Peri's principal theme, and the expressions of solace to be found in many places, such as the finale of the second section, a requiem in the form of a cradle song. The *Peri's* theme recurs in various forms in Nos 10, 13, 20, 23 and 25. A second recurring melodic figure is connected with the image of paradise (No 2) and can also be seen in No 11, and inverted in Nos 20 and 26. These two themes provide a musical continuity between the three separate sections with their different settings (India, Egypt and Syria) and their different dramatic characters, yet the sections themselves seem interchangeable, as was shown in 1843, during the official Schumann festival in Zwickau, when redemption at the end was effected by 'Blood' [from the noble warrior] rather than the tears of remorse.[68] Schumann's claim to a new genre was based on his use of choruses as groups to advance the action, choral fugues modelled on Handel – Mendelssohn's

St Paul had *lit the path* here (GS2,4) – but especially in his instrumentation. He used horns at all pitches, valve trumpets, alto, tenor and bass trombones and ophycleide, plus harp and a large percussion section. Opera at this time was dominated by the French and the Italians, so Schumann was setting out to give his work a specifically German sound, using a vernacular type of music, with the principle of repetition, appealing melodies without any coloratura, engaging refrains (No 18) and chorale sections (Nos 23 and 24) and using numbers that usually had three verses. The King of Saxony sent a golden snuff-box to thank Schumann for the score, while the King of Prussia sent a gold medal. The *Allgemeine Musikalische Zeitung* spoke for many in the audience as it enjoyed the 'melodies that linger in the ear' and prophesied that this work would certainly 'be welcomed by all choirs and larger private groups'.[69] It did not seem to cross Schumann's mind that his own oratorio might be a step towards the *false popularity* of which he had warned in his journal (GS2,248).

The rehearsals were extremely exhausting. Schumann called on his wife for help. 'Madame thundered out the whole piano score', David wrote to Mendelssohn in October, 'while he conducted with his lorgnette, producing a heavenly sort of beat, that I could not possibly translate into mere earthly terms, which is why I stayed by the piano.' Shortly before the performance David was a little more specific in his complaints: Schumann always held his baton up to his mouth when he was speaking, so none of the players could understand his directions, and the four orchestral rehearsals had been a waste of time.[70] Nevertheless, the oratorio was massively applauded at its first performance on 4 December 1843 with Livia Frege in the title role. Schumann, who conducted, received a laurel wreath. He was most pleased, however, that Mendelssohn thought the work 'very important and distinguished'.[71]

3 April marked the opening of the Leipzig Conservatory.

Mendelssohn had worked for two years to get this established, and it was the first institute of its kind in Germany, with some 40 students. The teachers included the best musicians in Leipzig: Mendelssohn, Schumann, David, Moritz Hauptmann (Kantor at St Thomas's Church), the organist Carl Ferdinand Becker, and later Moscheles and Gade. Schumann taught piano, composition and score-reading for three hours a week. Wasielewski, his biographer, who once took part in one of Schumann's lessons as a violin student, told how Schumann was silent the whole time. He was 'difficult to approach and uncommunicative' – he simply lacked the 'ability to make himself understood' (W322,323).

Schumann's music was gradually winning support in private circles. Interest was shown particularly in the string quartets, the piano quintet, the variations for two pianos, Op 46, and in his songs. In January 1843 Wieck suddenly invited his daughter to

The conservatory in Leipzig. Lithograph, c. 1850

Dresden to perform Schumann's quintet at his house. Two years before this Wieck had been sentenced in court for libel against Schumann, and this had been followed by unpleasant arguments over Clara's personal assets. Now she was pleased to receive the first conciliatory gesture from her father in a long time, and she visited him in February. Then at the end of the year, when Schumann had finally achieved success with the *Peri*, Wieck proposed a reconciliation, without any 'long explanation' (L2,13). In spite of their perceptible alienation the family celebrated Christmas together in Dresden. Their relationship remained distant.

The year 1843 had been the most successful so far, but Clara Schumann hinted that there had been 'little storms' in their

Clara and Marie
Schumann.
Daguerreotype,
c. 1844/45

marriage – *serious rows* according to Schumann (T3,253) – for which his wife bore the blame. The reason was her 'fretting' that she had to give up her concert tours (T2,269) although she considered she would now be able to travel again, following the birth of her second daughter, Elise, on 25 April 1843. Schumann himself was depressed, feeling exhausted as he often did when he had completed a major work, and he was fearful both of travelling, and of his *solitude* at home (T3,237) if Clara travelled without him. On the one hand, he showed remarkable understanding for Clara as an artist, and especially as a composer (although she did not see herself as such), but on the other, he held fast to the conventions of the bourgeoisie in the three virtues at the beginning of their marriage diary: *hard work, economy and loyalty* (T2,100). He was touched by his wife's compositions, *so gentle and so richly musical*, achieved despite her constant attention to household matters. Nevertheless he was firm in his insistence that her *chief occupation* was to be a mother (T2,255). Clara, had appealed to Mendelssohn about her *uncertainties* (L2,85) and it was he who finally persuaded Schumann to undertake the long planned concert tour to St Petersburg in January of the following year. The children would stay with Schumann's brother in Schneeberg for four and a half months. *Travel was a hardship*, and many difficulties were associated with the tour – the timing was unfortunate as the season in Moscow was really over and the nobility had mostly gone to the country – but nevertheless the tour was a success for Clara, whose profits exceeded 6,000 talers. There were opportunities to perform in Königsberg, Mitau and Dorpat, then four concerts in St Petersburg. She gave three performances in Moscow, and played benefit concerts where required. Although the concert halls were sometimes *rather empty*, the applause was often *enthusiastic* (T2,295, 298). Her programmes included Beethoven sonatas, pieces by Mendelssohn, Chopin, Liszt and Henselt, Bach and Scarlatti, even some of her own.

Only seldom did she play works by Schumann, since even Liszt had had 'such a great fiasco' with them that he confessed to 'losing heart' about including them in his programmes (Q145). In St Petersburg they were often invited to the Henselts, they met Pauline Viardot and the Romberg brothers, made music with the violinist Lvov and Count Wielhorski, and visited Schumann's uncle, the landowner and former regimental surgeon Carl Schnabel, near Tver. The Russian aristocracy was *obsessed with Italian opera* (Boe 401), but, apart from this, what they most wanted to hear was Mendelssohn. Nevertheless, there were opportunities to play Schumann's chamber music in private houses, especially the Piano Quintet, and Schumann conducted his Spring Symphony on one occasion at a soirée.

Schumann was ill almost constantly on this Russian tour. He suffered from heavy colds, rheumatic pains, dizzy spells, panic attacks and he spent many days in bed; the doctors spoke of a 'fever of the nerves'. The diary hardly conceals his own opposition to the tour. He complained of the *dreadful* hotel rooms, of the *impossible rush and tear*, *a terrible feeling* when crossing the Weichsel, of the *awful roads in an awful carriage*, and of the *barbaric* music in the Russian churches (T2, 281, 279, 291, 286). Clara later repeated much of his criticism word for word in her own travel report, as if she wanted to placate her husband by falling in with his opinions. On this tour he was just the husband of the artist, who could be overlooked in invitations to dinner or to court, or into whose hand money might discreetly be pressed, and he found this *insulting, hardly to be borne.* He added in the diary: *and Clara's behaviour too* (T2,294), though he did not say it to her face. He was often in a bad mood, seldom spoke in company and then only 'in a whisper' so that Clara had to answer 'any question for her husband', in French, 'with a Saxon accent' (Q144). The aristocracy always regarded the artist as a socially inferior being, so that Clara often felt as if she was some sort of 'strange animal being displayed' in this society (T2,327). Schumann read the second part of Goethe's *Faust* and copied one of the scenes intending to make a composition out of it, but he could not work. He went for walks by himself, passed his time writing long poems about the Kremlin and longed for home. On 24 May 1844 they finally returned to Leipzig. Schumann then suffered *after-effects from the journey* (E1,311). He was also missing Mendelssohn, who had left Leipzig at the end of November 1843, having received an offer from Friedrich Wilhelm IV to move to Berlin.

Schumann had been planning an opera for some time, though he searched in vain for a librettist. He had been working on the final scene from the second part of *Faust* and was considering turning this project into an oratorio (NF244). He therefore decided to give up his journalistic work to *devote himself entirely to composition* (NF241). Three years before this, while working on the symphonies, he had been complaining repeatedly about the *confounded journal* (T3,198) – his wife agreed that the 'fatal journal' took up too much of his time (T2,261). At the end of June he passed the editorship to Lorenz (NF241) – not without some qualms about the loss of his *regular work*. Lorenz had already covered for him during the tour of Russia. In November Franz Brendel became the proprietor of the *Neue Zeitschrift*. Another reason forcing Schumann to this step was illness. In the middle of August he suffered his most serious breakdown yet, and during the holiday he took afterwards to convalesce his situation deteriorated further. His doctor at the time reported that he had a phobia of high mountains, tall buildings, even metal tools and that he was fearful of medicines because he thought he might be poisoned. He was incapable either of working or listening to music. His misery was compounded by the fact that the 27-year-old Niels Gade had been appointed to succeed Mendelssohn rather than Schumann himself. Suddenly they decided to move to

Dresden. Clara, pregnant once more, hoped that they might receive some support from her parents. For Schumann, moving house was always an attempt to free himself from a crisis. So, on 8 December 1844 they gave their farewell matinée in Leipzig and moved five days later to Dresden.

Distant Places

Dresden has been described as 'a spacious city with Italianate towers, churches and palaces, the Florence of the north'.[72] The Zwinger contained wonderful art collections, there were vast houses for the nobility, while the wide flights of steps up to the Brühl Terraces, the great park around the Italian Palace and the Roman Catholic Cathedral represented the best in aristocratic cultural taste. Leipzig seemed provincially bourgeois by comparison. Clara and Robert Schumann lived in the Waisenhausstrasse, near the Kreuzkirche and not far from the Palace Gardens and the Brühl Terraces. Later they moved to the Reitbahnstrasse, where they had a larger apartment, but they were still in the old town. Ferdinand Hiller introduced the Schumanns into a social milieu dominated by painters and writers. Here they met the authors Berthold Auerbach and Otto Ludwig, the artists Eduard Bendemann and Julius Hübner, who each painted grand historical scenes as well as portraits, and the sculptor Ernst Rietschel. Schumann's medical advisor, Carl Gustav Carus, was also a member of this circle – he was a renowned natural scientist, doctor, painter and philosopher. The Schumanns missed their larger circle of friends in Leipzig, although they did gradually become closer to Eduard and Lida Bendemann. They spent a summer holiday with Major Serre on his estate near the city – he had been a friend for a long time – but this did little to dispel their feelings about the *secluded life* they were now leading (T3,381). Occasional visits from Mendelssohn, Gade, David, Verhulst and Moscheles only intensified their homesickness for Leipzig. When Mendelssohn died on 4 November 1847, and shortly afterwards Hiller moved to Düsseldorf, they felt even more isolated. Then again there were the Wieck's parties, where they had to admire the progress of Minna and Marie: Wieck's ambitions were now firmly fixed on Clara's half-sister, Marie, and his ward, Minna Schulz, who was destined for great things as a singer. Schumann found that the existing tension with Wieck increased because of Wieck's open admiration for Meyerbeer. This made Schumann feel that the new contact was a burden.

'Dresden is a musical backwater', Clara wrote in her diary (L2,95). Robert grumbled to Gade about the Dresden musicians – *the best example of Philistines* (Boe408). They are *Dyed in the wool* he wrote to Mendelssohn (NF250). Interest was predominantly in the Opera, where Richard Wagner had been appointed Hofkapellmeister in 1842. Nothing could be done with the Hofkapelle (court orchestra), since it was under the direction of Reissiger, described by Schumann as a *Justemilieuiste* (NF66, 250). There were no regular concerts, and contemporary works were almost never played, with the exception of *only one symphony by Beethoven each year, and then it would be with over-embellished playing ad libitum by the orchestra* (NF252). Ferdinand Hiller, who conducted the men's chorus known as 'Liedertafel' seemed to be 'the only one . . . with whom one could have a proper conversation about music' (L2,104). Schumann had dedicated his piano concerto to Hiller, and was of the opinion that *nature had endowed this man as one of* her very favourites (GS2,375), considering that in many ways, in the opinion of Schumann, he resembled Mendelssohn. Through Hiller there was soon a prospect for Robert and Clara Schumann to appear in public. Schumann was invited onto the committee to inaugurate regular subscription concerts in Dresden. The orchestra consisted of both military and city musicians, so they looked to Leipzig for support. Hiller and Schumann were to take turns conducting. The orchestra was quite competent, *the wind instruments were excellent*, Schumann reported to Leipzig, but unfortunately they played mostly for an audience of aristocrats. I fear we often *played too good for them* (NF253).

The great musical event during their first year in Dresden was the first performance of *Tannhäuser*, on 19 October [1845]. Wagner had known Schumann for many years, having written reports for the *Neue Zeitschrift*, and he had repeatedly begged Schumann to review *Rienzi* and the *Flying Dutchman*. 'My dearest friend, let us stick together', he had suggested.[73] Schumann held back, since he liked neither the operas nor their composer, with his enormous *torrents of words* (T2,398). As a musician, Schumann thought Wagner *often a complete amateur*, with no *sense of form and harmony* (E2,195, 194); he was certainly *full of ideas and extremely bold*, but he was lacking in solid craftsmanship, *in four part choral expertise*, to the extent that Schumann recognized the parallel fifths and octaves in the score of *Tannhäuser*, sent to him by the composer (NF252). After the first performance of the opera, however, Schumann modified his opinion. *On the stage everything seemed different*; he felt *taken with many things*, he thought it was *deeper, more original and 100 times better* than Wagner's earlier operas, and found the instrumentation *excellent*, although his doubts were confirmed by *several musical trivialities* (NF254,256). Schumann must have felt very downcast that Wagner had succeeded where he himself had failed – for three years the subject of his *morning and evening prayers of an artist had been: German opera* (NF220). It was not the first time he had felt defeated by Wagner: he had been 'overshadowed' in 1833 by his C major Symphony, as Clara Wieck had noted at the time. Then one evening in the middle of December 1845, Wagner read to a group of guests at the Hiller's house from his text for *Lohengrin* (the opera that would bring him fame as an operatic reformer), and once again Schumann realised that he had been scooped in his subject material, and had *to throw* this own project for *King Arthur away* (NF255).

Schumann became seriously ill in August 1844, and did not recover until 1846. He suffered from *great lassitude* and *weak nerves*, panic attacks and dizziness, headaches, *something wrong with my ears and weakness in my eyes*, that had also afflicted him in Moscow (T3, 403, 380, 415, 391). He hoped that he would find relief in *steel baths* (a spa treatment using iron carbonates) during the summer, and in August 1845 he tried *plunge baths*, but without success. His *horrific weakness* (T2,393) would not even allow a visit to Bonn for the dedication of the Beethoven Memorial. Schumann seemed old before his time, he became clumsy in his movements and his silence was worrying: *who are you – we hardly recognise you! But I recognise all of you*, runs an entry in his diary

In order to be able to study the use of the organ pedal, Schumann hired a pedal piano in April 1845. The instrument fascinated him so much, that he composed *Sketches* op. 58 and *Studies for Pedal Piano* op. 56 on it

(T2,400). The Schumanns had stopped writing a diary of their marriage. Mostly now Schumann just noted down short comments in his *household book*, alongside careful lists of income and expenses. He was thirty five years old by this time, and considered writing his memoirs (T3,416). Privy Councillor Carus had advised a walk each morning, so sometimes he took little Marie with him. He was *happy with the child* (T3,383) as she walked along holding his hand, but everything else was too much for him – both *joy and pain* would *debilitate* him equally (Boe 413).

In January 1845 he and Clara had begun a *busy study of fugue*, and he hoped that this would give him strength. He decided to create a tribute to Bach in six organ fugues, Op 60, *on the name BACH*, the last of these in November 1845. Like the *Studies for Pedal Piano* [Op 56] and the four Piano Fugues, Op 72, these organ fugues were an attempt to find relief through working to strict contrapuntal rules. Some of this can be seen in the retrograde mood of the theme in the fourth and fifth BACH fugues.

His sketch for the C major symphony, in December 1845, shows that composition within such strict rules did actually help Schumann to throw off the weakness from which he had been suffering throughout the year. He had written to Mendelssohn in the autumn that *for days now there has been a drumming and trumpeting in my head (trumpet in C)* (NF249) – he was referring to the fanfare motif which was to introduce his new symphony in C major, reminiscent of the opening of Haydn's Symphony in D major, No 104, and placing Schumann's work firmly in the tradition of musical history. It is also quite evident how hard he was trying to create forms that had longevity. Schumann's identity crisis, his experience of how far personality is dependent on its period, finds artistic expression in discontinuities, abrupt pauses and in a return to the past. The slow introduction itself indicates his search for a form, with its permanent circular movement, the fanfare indicating a distant objective, its uncertain tonality and its short motifs lacking length and substance. Even the themes of the Allegro seem provisional. The main theme, derived from the circular melody of the introduction, feels as if it has been created laboriously, with sharp dotted rythyms and rhythmic dislocations – the melody goes nowhere. The development reinforces this feeling of dissociation; material from the second theme and the final section is developed, but the main theme is absent. It is only just at the end, in the coda, that there is a breakthrough – and not with the main theme, but with the motto, more of a reminder than a firm statement. The Scherzo expresses an attitude to life more associated with the 'sufferings' of the Kapellmeister Kreisler: 'Crazy, crazy apparition, why are you shaking me so'.[74] This feeling of dizziness, the fear of disorientation, is expressed in a wild, tense section at breathless semiquaver speed, where the tonality of C major is only 'established' after 82 bars. The motto in the concluding coda vanquishes the 'apparition'. This movement, with its two trios, contains several strongly contrasting sections, but the surprisingly unusual transitional passages to the scherzo show that in their musical substance they are closely related to it. The triplets of the first trio dispel tension while the second trio seems to have escaped the fast speed elsewhere. This music is based on the severe style of Bach, as shown in the BACH quotation (bars 257-262) and the contrapuntal writing. The Adagio is in itself a tribute to Bach, with its elegiac C minor melody, whose first four notes quote the largo from the Trio Sonata of the Musical Offering. There are elements of the baroque style also in the polyphonic voice leading, the expressive melodic intervals and the fugato of the central section. It is, however, chiefly the personal *sounds of pain* (NF300), as Schumann described them, that can be heard in this symphony: in the chromatic harmony, the syncopation of the chordal accompaniment, the sensitive dynamics, and in the almost painfully high writing for the violins. The finale opens with an attempt to reconcile the various musical elements into a whole. The wind motif that follows is reminiscent of the opening of Mendelssohn's Italian Symphony, the fast runs of the second group are in extreme contrast to the obsessiveness of the Scherzo, while the elegiac melody of the Adagio appears transformed into an almost dance-like motif in the second group. The development (bars 118ff) puts an end to the élan of the exposition, with extended sequences of the soaring motif, with minor tonalities and with a strictly imitative section. The positive mood of the opening is not maintained, despite short climaxes. The motto seems to evoke a new thematic form (bars 211ff): the inversion of the melody from the adagio, ending with a falling movement, indicates a fading away. The music seems to break off in uncertainty with a general pause, giving strength to the creation of a final apotheosis. The symphony's themes are not strong enough to dominate: the recurring quotation 'Bear them hence, these songs' from Beethoven's cycle *An die ferne Geliebte*, Op 98 No 4, shows that 'salvation' is no longer possible at the present time. The quotation is combined with the motto, the main theme and motifs from the introduction, into an emphatic climax where once again there is a utopian moment from the finale of the Ninth Symphony, when Schumann (bars 544-551) hints at the chorus in Beethoven's finale (bars 806 ff).

Schumann *only* made *small progress* (T3,414) with the instrumentation, and it was almost a year before the Symphony, Op 61, was ready for its first performance in the Leipzig Gewandhaus, on 5 November 1846. In this work of a *dark period* you can particularly *hear* the melancholy that Schumann had composed when he was *half ill* (NF300). It was not a success.

On 4 December 1845 the first performance of the Piano Concerto, with Clara as soloist, and the revised Overture, Op 52, were occasions for joy. They were performed in the Hôtel de Saxe with Hiller conducting. Nevertheless, this was a period of financial insecurity for the Schumanns. Clara was giving piano lessons and her occasional concert performances brought in some income. The profits from the tour of Russia, were, however, soon spent. Their [third] daughter, Julie [born 11 March 1845], was followed a mere eleven months later, in February 1846, by the birth of their first son, Emil, who died in June of the following year. For Clara the *certainty* of yet another pregnancy, in July 1846, felt like a misfortune; she was *pleased* when she appeared to have a miscarriage at Nordeney during their summer holiday in July and August (T3,284,285). Clara was ill for weeks after this. By the end of 1846 she had recovered sufficiently to contemplate an extended concert tour once again. They set off on 24 November with their two older children, Marie and Elise, for a two-month tour to Vienna. They well remembered the great success Clara had had in that city nine years before, and were looking forward to the tour, hoping that perhaps they might make a home there one day. This time, however, Clara's concerts were poorly attended. She included in her programme the Piano Concerto in G major by Beethoven, with her own cadenza, Schumann's Piano Quintet, his Variations, Op 46, her own Scherzo, Op 14, as well as music by Chopin, Mendelssohn and Scarlatti – 'too good', they heard people say, 'the audience could not understand them' (L2,144). There was a very small audience for the third concert, where Schumann conducted his own First Symphony and Piano Concerto in A minor. The applause was cool, and what was worse, the costs far outweighed the income. At the last concert, on the other hand, Clara earned back all their costs plus a profit of more than 300 talers – but the enthusiasm of the public was only directed towards the singing of Jenny Lind, who had spontaneously offered her friendship and support. The *Allgemeine Theaterzeitung* reported that 'people came just to see and hear her' (T3, 737). The entry in Schumann's diary read: *Clara in tears* (T3,340). Such bitter disappointment could not even be dispelled by the Farewell Matinée, on 15 January 1847, which was attended by such old friends as Jenny Lind, Vesque von Püttlingen, Grillparzer as well as Eichendorff and Stifter. There were concerts in Brünn and Prague on the way home, then Clara, Robert and the children arrived back in Dresden on 4 February. Their son was seriously ill, but they set off again the following week for Berlin. A performance of Schumann's oratorio, *Paradise and the Peri*, was scheduled at the Singakademie, but conditions there were so bad that it was not a success, despite many exhausting rehearsals. The Piano Quintet, Op 44, was played at two of Clara's concerts, and the Piano Quartet, Op 47 was performed at a matinée. The critics praised the pianist, but were reserved about Robert Schumann's works. In Berlin they met Fanny Hensel (Mendelssohn's sister), Pauline Viardot and Henriette Sontag, and thought they might consider living in this city, rather than Dresden or Vienna. Fanny Hensel, to whom Clara felt especially drawn, was the deciding factor in their decision to move to Berlin, but her death, in May 1847, destroyed their plans.

Following a period of *gloomy moods* (NF319), Schumann wrote his first Piano Trio in D minor, the dark key of his late works. It begins like a nocturne, in a low register with restless triplets in the bass. The rising fourths of the main melody and its resistance against the measure are signs of an attempt to liberate himself. The rhythmic energy of the melody in the transitional section demonstrates Schumann's self-contemplation and reliance on his own strengths, as do the speech-like recitatives, and especially the development section that follow, where a new theme is heard as from a distance. The sul ponticello playing of unison strings, the static piano chords in a high register, together with echoes of the lydian mode, create the impression that time is standing still and the listener is hearing the past. The strength for change that grows from self-contemplation, can be seen in

Jenny Lind's concert in Hamburg. Caricature, 1845

the coda, where for a moment the main theme moves from D minor to D major. The intention of the first movement appears again in the Scherzo, in the predominance of sharp dotted rhythms and the tense dissonance between harsh accompanying chords and the melody. This theme is derived from the development motif of the first movement, and appears as a variation in the trio. The third movement is linked to the first through the recitative, and here song-form and variations are overlayed – the formal relationship is clear from the first bar, in which the opening theme appears once again. A monologue develops, a sort of prose without periodic structure, freely jumping between keys, held together only by the dense polyphonic texture. When the opening theme develops into the rondo-like theme of the finale in D major, to be played *with fire*, the music reaches its destination. Here the second subject and the theme of the development section (bars 172 ff) are related to the first movement, while the trio of the scherzo reappears in inversion. The imitative passage of bars 230 ff refers back once again to the polyphonic principle of the first and third movements, as Schumann applies his studies of fugue, made in 1845.

Clara immediately tried out the new trio with David and Grabau, and later with her regular trio partners, Franz and Friedrich Schubert. Schumann wrote two further works, Op 80 and Op 110, for piano, violin and cello, a combination he had experimented with five years earlier in the *Phantasiestücken*.

In early July Clara and Robert Schumann travelled to Zwickau where his old teacher Kuntsch and the local organist Emanuel Klitzsch had arranged a festival in honour of Schumann, and *for the benefit of those suffering distress in the Erzgebirge* (E2,22). The composer conducted a performance of his Symphony in C major, his Piano Concerto and the choral song *Beim Abschied zu singen*. It became a little 'folk festival' (L2,169) with serenades, odes of honour and a torchlight procession – a modest recompense for previous reversals.

During the years he spent in Dresden Schumann had been looking out for any position that would give him *a secure and respectable employment* (E2,34). In July 1847 he applied for a position as director of the Conservatory in Vienna, the following year for the succession of Gade in Leipzig, and finally he hoped, in vain, that he would be appointed second Hofkapellmeister in Dresden to replace Wagner, who had fled the city in 1849. At the end of October 1847 he did at least succeed Hiller as conductor of the Liedertafel, and shortly afterwards he founded another Choral Society. Schumann was soon to give up directing the Liedertafel, fed up with the *continuous 6/4 chords of the men's chorus style* (NF294). The weekly rehearsals, concerts, festivals and occasional parties in country houses with his mixed choir were a welcome break from his solitary writing. Their repertoire included choruses from Bach's *St John Passion*, from Handel's *Jephtha* and Beethoven's *Missa Solemnis*, as well as a capella music by Palestrina and works by Cherubini, Mendelssohn and Gade. Schumann also included a considerable number of his own songs, such as the final chorus from *Faust*, his *Requiem für Mignon*, and the motet *Verzweifle nicht im Schmerzenstal*. This regular work with the choir, plus two composition students[75] and the progress he was continuing to make on his opera *Genoveva*, gave Schumann some security; he was *happy and hard-working* during this year (T3,449), as he was always reminding himself in his diary. He was hoping that with *Genoveva* he would finally be writing *Zukunftsmusik* in a genre that would bring him wide publicity.

Schumann had contemplated writing an opera as early as 1831, and since that time he had considered various different subjects, but always hesitated. He discovered Hebbel's play *Genoveva* in the spring of 1847, sketching an overture at the beginning of April. In May Robert Reinick, a painter and writer, produced two acts of libretto that Schumann found *dreadfully sentimental* (NF273), so he wrote to Hebbel requesting corrections and suggestions from him. When Hebbel came to visit him in July 1847, Schumann was almost tongue-tied, he was so overcome at the *great honour* that had been *done to his house*. Hebbel left feeling he had been duped (T2,421). Schumann was therefore left to write his own libretto, sometimes stumbling over the rhymes. He took parts from Ludwig Tieck's tragedy *Leben und Tod der heiligen Genoveva*, but otherwise he followed Hebbel. Schumann *detested the vulgar style of operatic texts* in which Grand opéra was traditionally written, and wrote tempo markings and stage directions into his score explicitly in German. Like Weber and Marschner before him, he wanted to impress by other means than coloratura in his opera (NF268, E2,68). There is a natural simplicity to the vocal parts, songs and choruses use folk elements, arias resemble Lieder and even the recitative is different. One example of how Schumann successfully introduced folk song into a dramatic scene is the duet *Wenn ich ein Vöglein wär* (If I were a little bird), in which Golo, *forgetting himself*, 'behaves erratically', so that his part develops a momentum of its own and introduces the dramatic section *Im leidenschafflichen Tempo* (with a passionate tempo). Nevertheless, this opera still has much in common with Grand opéra, in its invocation of the devil, supernatural apparitions, the motif of the innocent accused who then seeks refuge in the cross. The choral scenes with which the opera opens show that Schumann had studied Wagner's scores – Bishop Hidulfus summons the faithful to a holy mission, just like King Heinrich in *Lohengrin*; Schumann knew from *Tannhäuser* how to exploit the three dimensional sound effect of a chorus approaching and retreating into the distance (this device is used in Act 1 and Act 4), and the interweaving of the scenes makes this opera resemble a music drama. On the other hand, the repeated motifs are not really leitmotifs with a clear cut symbolic meaning, as used by Wagner: here the unity of the 21 scenes is created by constant variation of the motifs and intervals. The *Gaunerlied* (Rogue's Song) is shown in retrospect to have been a variant of the central section of Genoveva's aria, No 16, *Wie wird die Luft von Tönen wach* (what lovely music sounds all about); both are also different manifestations of Siegfried's horn motif. A small number of patterns recur in many variations, such as the motif of the falling fifth, first associated with Golo, then reappearing in the chorale, in Margarethe's mocking song and in Siegfried's song. It is the motif of the fourth, in particular, that appears in so many guises. Sublime and subtle references can be made in this way, as for instance in the final duet between Siegfried and Genoveva (No 19) that echoes their farewell (No 3), or where her fear of the drunken servants (*Welches rohes Singen!* Such Rough Singing!) is transformed by the light of the magic mirror, in its third image, into *Sei verschwiegen, dunkle Nacht* (Be Secluded, Dark Night).

Links such as these, however, are almost useless on the operatic stage, as they cannot be immediately heard and recognised.

Once again, as in *Paradise and the Peri*, it is the 'holy spirits' who must redeem the ruined world. 'The saints are they, that storm the heavens/ To create Paradise anew' runs the final commentary by Bonifatius in Tieck's version. In the opera, Golo's acknowledgement of his guilt, the catastrophe in Hebbel's drama,[76] is dropped, and the Christian crusade is never questioned, as it had been by Hebbel in his scene with the Jews and in Tristan's story. The central figure in the opera is no longer Golo alone, but also Genoveva, the incarnation of the Madonna – for the young Schumann the image of womanhood. Both of Genoveva's arias are in the form of prayers. Hebbel's lines: 'This woman . . . gives life to sin' (line 833f) cannot be applied to Schumann's *Genoveva*. Whereas Hebbel's *Genoveva* undergoes dreadful martyrdom, suffering 'as much as any human being can

Scene from the 4th act from the opera *Genoveva*

bear' (1 2891), the sufferings of Schumann's protagonist in the opera merely arouse pathos. Her Passion is indicated in the verses of the chorale in the first scene of the opera, a sort of cantata, while the finale of Act 2 is reminiscent of Bach's Passion music. Siegfried's invitation *Kommt Alle mit in's Schloss* (Come into the castle, all of you), provides the *lieto fine* [happy ending] of a fairy-tale – incongruous after the terrible injustice that has preceded it. The many shouts of 'Hail' from those who were previously barbarians also beggars belief. The jubilation here is also for Siegfried, who has assumed much of the guilt himself, blinded by the demands of honour and apparently justified by a superstitious ritual. The nameless joy at the end of the opera therefore has a false ring to it, quite unlike the ending of Fidelio. Margarethe's attempt to set matters right is another example of reconciliation in this opera. Schumann gave this Mephistophelian figure a modern procedure that Liszt would later adopt in his own *Faust Symphony* – an ironic distortion. Golo's elegiac falling fifth motif is caricatured by Margarethe in her mocking song (No 7); she drives Golo to evil in a seductive romance, quoting the second bar from the farewell scene between Genoveva and Siegfried. Golo, 'this ardent, rushing character',[77] is portrayed in the main theme of the overture with a broken melodic line, with high notes, obsessively repeated against an unstable metric framework. His grief that he cannot be a hero like Siegfried, nor find his own place, is expressed in the motif of the falling fifth, while the unresolved chord of a minor ninth, with which the opera begins, and which runs as a motif throughout, becomes a symbol for the pain of the character who says, in Hebbel's drama, 'I am an open sore' (1 715). After Golo has left to roam the world at large (No 17), his unnamed misfortune is expressed in music alone – in an unusually bold harmonic sequence, a chord of the minor ninth followed by a chord of fourths. The misunderstanding between Golo's passionate avowal and Genoveva's cries of fear in scene nine acquires greater poignancy by being cast in the form of a traditional love duet. Golo's *madness* as he loses touch with reality is immediately obvious when his passionate singing of the *joys of love* are set against Genoveva's calls for help. It is the word *bastard* that jolts him back into reality, conscious of his own worthlessness. This is followed by silence, an inability to speak; then Golo's stammering (*that word struck deep*) repeats the steps of seconds from the beginning of the main theme in the overture. His curse of Genoveva, slow, pianissimo, with the hollow sound of broken diminished seventh chords, is that of someone who is already condemned; as the scene ends the flutes become slower and descend in lower registers – playing the music of death. There is a considerable lapse in the characterisation when this broken man immediately appears alert and inventive in his duet with Drago that follows. He continues to sink into a tone of melancholy introspection, driven 'to the greatest depths by sin' (l 1695) – again a contradiction, that is perhaps the more touching just because Schumann saw himself in Golo, thereby *writing a part of his own life* into the opera (NF 314).

At this time Schumann often talked with Wagner. He borrowed the score of *Lohengrin*, and in August he read Wagner the text of *Genoveva*, though he was rather upset at Wagner's criticisms. At the concert celebrating the tercentenary of the royal court orchestra in September 1848 it was brought home to Schumann that he counted for nothing as a composer – in contrast to Wagner, or even to Reissiger. Dresden composers, both past and present, featured on the programme of this concert, but the name of Schumann was missing.

In July of 1848, the Year of Revolution, Schumann reread Byron's Manfred. By choosing the existential doubts of this isolated character as a subject for his composition at this time, we can assume that it is not a clear indication of the distant view Schumann took of the hopes raised by the revolution. Byron had intended this play as a sort of monologue, to be read rather than performed. Schumann cut much of Suckow's German translation, inverted the scene order here and there, but left the words

Robert Schumann. Charcoal drawing by Eduard Bendemann (1859) after a Daguerreotype of 1850

unchanged. Apart from the overture he composed music for 15 scenes, where spoken text predominated. In *Manfred* Byron had presented the freedom and self-determination of the individual as autonomy that cannot be sustained because it leads to self-destruction. His character is elitist and monomaniacal, incapable of close relationships, cold in his 'terrible' talent, to be contrasted with the 'harmony' of creation – an early fore-runner for figures in the works of Sartre and Camus. Schumann did not take Byron's radical point of view. For Schumann redemption is what counts, salvation through the *Ewig-Weibliche* (the Eternally Feminine), as in the *Chorus mysticus* from his *Faust* of the previous year. The unusual way he set the accidentals in E flat major when the main key is that of E flat minor, demonstrates this. Salvation by a woman is also a biographical theme for Schumann. He had hoped that Ernestine von Fricken would *save* him (Bw96), and for a long time he believed this of Clara Wieck. Byron's Manfred finds his 'peace' in the certainty that there is nothing beyond death, but Schumann gave Manfred's words (No 12) quite a different meaning in the music to which he set them. The quotation (bar 7) of *Since I saw him* (from Op 42 No 1), placed as it is where silence becomes music, indicates that he will be reunited with Astarte, and hence this is the basis for the 'peace' he has found. The closing scene presents a definite deviation from Byron's dramatic poem. For Byron, death is the gateway to the void – 'Whither, I dread to think', the words of the Abbot at the end. In Schumann's final scene the requiem chorus sings of eternal light (*luceat eis*) while simultaneously flutes and oboes play Astarte's melody in a bright E flat major, the key in which the work ends.

The sparse means Schumann used to link his scenes with music can be seen in the three note motif with which Nos 9 and 11 begin. A minor second is followed by a broken minor triad, turning to the major at the appearance of Astarte; this motif also forms the upbeat to the main theme of the overture, and returns in various forms in other scenes, emphasising the monologue nature of the work. The setting as melodrama (spoken word with musical accompaniment) in nine of the 15 scenes belongs with Schumann's later experiments in the *Balladen*, Op 106 and Op 122. He wanted to create *something new and incredible* (NF350) in his use of an 18th century form – it was one with which Wagner, Liszt and Berlioz also experimented. He used melodrama in various ways, setting speech to the accompaniment of the orchestra, a single instrument, a chamber group, or an off-stage choir with organ. In the last two numbers the voice speaks sometimes with a given rhythm, as in the *Sprechgesang* in the melodrama of the early 20th century.[78]

In the overture Schumann created the last in his series of self-portraits that run from the figures in *Carnaval* to the character of Golo. Here he is at his most revealing in his use of two questing themes that fail to find a destination; in the disparity of their tonal relationship (E flat minor/F sharp minor); in the restlessness of the *passionate tempos*, with their syncopation and strong accents; in the melancholy of the dark harmony and the dominating falling seconds; in the painful dissonances of the suspensions and chords of the seventh; but also in the strength of the upbeats and the rhythmic energy; even the turn motif for *Eusebius* (bar 68, 97) comes back again. All the themes and motifs of this monothematic sonata form are derived from the semitone, both rising and falling in bar 2 of the introduction, combined with the dissonances of the seven chords of the relative keys. The secondary theme is built from inverted intervals taken from the main theme; this three note up-beat motif, repeated five times at the opening, and recurring in numerous scenes, corresponds to the three note sequence at the beginning of the second subject (bar 52 f). The close relationship of both themes reflects that of Manfred and Astarte, his more beautiful counterpart, similar to him 'in all her features', whose grief is expressed in the chromatic falling line of the low notes in the second subject. The coda is unusual. Here the forced rising scale motif is followed by a fragment of the second subject in E flat minor, piano, with pale brass calls as accompaniment, until the music, *becoming ever weaker*, reaches the Introduction. Here the second subject, now in E flat major, can be heard in the solo flute, like a momentary farewell, before the dissociation of the main theme can be recognised, pianissimo and without any low basses. This conclusion holds no promise of redemption; it is rather a portrayal of defeat.

Schumann wrote several short piano pieces for the seventh birthday of his daughter Marie, on 1 September 1848. They soon became a Christmas album, the *Album für die Jugend* (Album for the Young), Op 68. These 43 miniatures, with their descriptive titles, were the first works Schumann wrote for children and young people. They were followed by *Lieder für die Jugend* (Song Album for the Young), Op 79, two cycles for piano duet, Op 85 and Op 109, and the *Clavier-Sonaten für die Jugend* (Piano Sonatas for the Young), Op 118, dedicated to his three eldest daughters. There is a gradual progression in technique from easy to more difficult, while the didactic aim of the Album can be seen in the similarities to works by Bach, Mendelssohn and Gade – originally it also contained arrangements of pieces by Beethoven, Mozart and Weber.[79] Schumann formulated his teaching principles in his *Musikalische Haus-und Lebensregeln* (Musical Rules for Home and Life), and his initial intention was that they be applied to the individual pieces. These rules were based on a progressive idea of instrumental teaching that included ear training, harmony and counterpoint, reading old keys and a knowledge of history of music, as well as a moral education.

Whatever work he may have been doing, Schumann still followed the political events of 1848 closely. *A great revolutionary year. Read more newspapers than books*, he jotted in his little reading

Title page by Ludwig Richter of an early and not-yet-complete edition of *Album For Young People*

notebook (Boe 441). The entry in his diary *Völkerfrühling* (People's Spring) (T3, 456), suggests that he knew the popular propaganda, and perhaps also the poem by Otto Ludwig with the refrain: 'Freedom! oh people's spring!' Schumann had been in favour of freedom of the press and a written constitution for many years, although he was not insensitive to the *favours of those in power* (T2,242) – Metternich, and the Kings of Saxony and Prussia. While still at school he had written: *Political freedom is perhaps the real midwife for poetry* (T1,77), and he had followed the liberation movements in the summer of 1830 with sympathy. Now hopes were aroused by news from Berlin and Vienna about the uprisings in March and the retreat of Metternich; *great times*, Schumann wrote in his diary (T3,455). Immediately after the March uprisings he composed *Drei Freiheitsgesänge: Zu den Waffen, Schwarz-Rot-Gold* and *Deutscher Freiheitsgesang* (Three Songs of Liberation: To Arms, Black-Red-Gold and German Song of Liberation). But he was not one of those Dresden musicians who suddenly turned 'completely political', like the music director Röckel, who wrote about 'arming the people', or Wagner, who held lectures (T3,768) as a member of the *Vaterlandsverein* (Fatherland Club). Schumann may have hoped in 1848 that even *Dresden, something of a political backwater*, would *not be able to resist the great common surge* (NF284), but he was nevertheless frightened when the revolution did actually reach Dresden the following year. While there were confrontations in the streets, on 3 and 4 May 1849, barricades were erected and fighting raged between the revolutionaries and soldiers armed with cannons, who shot at the citizens, causing the first fatalities, Schumann was busy composing his *Kinderlieder* (Songs for Children) (T3,490). Fearful that he might be drafted into the 'watch', Schumann fled with his wife and Marie to the Maxen estate – Clara had to go back and fetch the other three children, including one-year-old Ludwig, who they had left behind in their haste. Although she was seven months pregnant, she set out at three the next morning on her hazardous and exhausting journey, with only two other women to accompany her. The revolution was crushed, with the help of two Prussian regiments, leaving the town devastated, the opera house burned to the ground, while prisoners were held in the Frauenkirche. Clara wrote in her diary of 'dreadful atrocities'. 'When will the time come when all men will have equal rights?' she asked. There was a warrant out for Wagner, who had 'made speeches from the steps of the town hall' (L2,189, 190). Schumann, on the other hand, was writing the music for the *Wandelnde Glocke*: spinning a cocoon to isolate himself from the dreadful events *breaking in from outside* (NF 302). They spent the following four weeks in Bad Kreischa, where they lived *in deepest peace: and so we spin and spin away until we have spun ourselves into our web* (NF 304, 321). Schumann composed four marches, Op 76) *not old Dessau ones, but more republican* (E2,90). The title page pointedly carries the year 1849.

1849 was the year in which Schumann composed the most works. These included the *Scenes from Goethe's Faust*, two large-scale concertos: *Introduction and Allegro appassionato* for piano and orchestra, Op 92 and the *Konzertstück for four Horns*, Op 86. He was experimenting with various combinations of instruments in

Revolts in Dresden, May 1849

his chamber works (clarinet, horn, oboe and cello with piano). There were several volumes of *Romances and Ballades*, song cycles, the melodrama *Schöne Hedwig* and the songs from Goethe's *Wilhelm Meister*, and choral works such as the Motet Op 93. His hopes for a breakthrough with his opera facilitated this work. Nevertheless, Schumann was playing an almost negligible role in the musical life of Dresden. Large-scale instrumental works, such as the Symphony in C major, the Concert Pieces, Op 86 and Op 92, and the *Genoveva* overture were all performed in the Leipzig Gewandhaus, not in Dresden. The Schumanns were not even given free entry to the Court Theatre, as was usually offered to well-known artists. Schumann himself remarked on his own artistic isolation, dating from the death of Mendelssohn and his gradual estrangement from Chopin, and particularly since Liszt, with whom he had had an altercation in 1848 over a derogatory remark about Mendelssohn, had aligned himself firmly with Wagner. The musicians with whom he was friendly were not necessarily those whom he wished *as critics* (NF293). He had never been close to Berlioz, mostly owing to language difficulties, while the composers of whom he had written as the avant garde in his last journal article *Neue Bahnen* were mostly insignificant; the works of the better known of these composers, Robert Franz, Niels Gade and Theodor Kirchner, were in smaller genres.

Schumann had received an offer in December 1849 to succeed Hiller as musical director in Düsseldorf. For a long time he remained undecided about this, as he was still hoping his opera *Genoveva* would lead to a turn in his fortunes. The first performance, originally scheduled for February 1850, had to be postponed in favour of Meyerbeer's *Le prophète*. Schumann's laconic comment on the performance in Dresden was: *In the evening to the Prophet – Oh!* (T3,517). Robert and Clara made concert tours to Bremen, Hamburg and Berlin to fill in the time before the premiere. At the end of March Schumann decided to take the position in Düsseldorf, receiving three months salary in May, plus 50 talers towards his removal expenses. They therefore went to Leipzig for the first performance of *Genoveva* with confidence. People were clearly expecting a small sensation, because Spohr, Hiller, Gade, Liszt and Schumann's old teacher Kuntsch had all come. The opera was withdrawn after only three performances, on 25, 28 and 30 June. Brendel reported in the *Neue Zeitschrift* that 'it was not lacking in external honours' 'but that it lacked inner warmth, the enthusiasm' of the audience; although he praised 'the heights of the inspiration', he could not conceal his impression that it was 'a monotonous sequence'. Christian Lobe, at that time editor of the *Allgemeine Musikalische Zeitung* was more explicit: the opera had 'decidedly not appealed to the general public' (Q 165ff). A few days later Schumann suffered an attack of *dizziness* and relapsed into *grief* (T3, 531). The months until they moved to Düsseldorf were taken up with organising his manuscripts, correcting, and composing several songs. Although the men in his choir preferred to go 'to the illuminations on the Vogelwiese' rather than attend rehearsals (L2,220), the Choral Society gave a serenade for their conductor on 30 August on the Brühl Terrace. One of the guests at this party reported that Schumann 'behaved disrespectfully': 'he said of the wine poured into his glass by Bendemann, that it tasted bad' (T3,786). There was no official farewell celebration, and when Robert and Clara Schumann left Dresden on 1 September 1850 it was as if they had never been there.

'The mountains whirl, spinning around me – I grow blind'[80]

Schumann and his family arrived in Düsseldorf on the evening of 2 September 1850. They were welcomed at the railway station by Hiller and the directors of the concert society; the 'Liedertafel' sang and they found their room at the hotel Breidenbacher Hof had been decorated with flowers and laurels. Düsseldorf, then a small town, expected great things from the Schumanns, as is evident from the honours bestowed on them. The orchestra serenaded them in the hotel, and at the end of their first week the concert committee gave a reception in their honour, beginning with a concert at which the *Genoveva* overture was played, along with several of Schumann's songs and the second part of *Paradise and the Peri*. This was followed by a banquet and a ball. In his new position as music director Schumann was responsible for conducting the orchestra and the *Allgemeine Musikverein* in ten subscription concerts each winter, as well as directing four programmes of music for churches of St Maximilian and St Lambertus during the year. The orchestra had been well trained by Schumann's predecessors Mendelssohn, Rietz and Hiller, and was 'quite excellent for a small town', as Clara remarked (L2,228). *We perform the most beautiful music*, Schumann wrote to Dresden in December 1850 (E2,130). They played 'classical' works, predominantly by Bach and Beethoven, as well as those of contemporary composers such as Mendelssohn, Gade and Hiller. On Schumann's initiative, young composers were also encouraged to submit new works for performance. In his first season alone Schumann premiered six of his own compositions, mostly from manuscript: they were choral pieces, an overture and his Third Symphony, Op 97. It is interesting, however, that he never conducted any Berlioz, Liszt or Wagner. In 1848 he had pronounced Gade's *Comola* to be *the most important work of the present period* (NF 286); on the other hand he spoke of the music of the *Neudeutsche Schule* as the *Weimar Evangelicals* (E2,178). Liszt, accompanied by the Princess Wittgenstein, visited the Schumann family at the beginning of September 1851, once again 'turning the household upside down'. Schumann was fascinated still with Liszt's 'demonic dash' but his compositions were 'such terrible stuff', as Clara put it, and Schumann's reserve and silence 'embarrassed' Liszt (L2,263 f).

At that time the Schumanns were living in the Königsallee. They had moved from their first apartment, on the corner of the Alleestrasse and Grabenstrasse because the street noise was too much for them, making Schumann 'nervous and agitated' (L2,227). In April 1852 they had to move yet again because the house was to be sold. They lived for a short time in the Herzogstrasse, but Schumann complained of the street noise and *the terrible disturbances by the neighbours* (T3,598), so in autumn 1852 they rented two floors in the Bilker Strasse (today's number 15), so that Clara could practise even when her husband was working at home.

Hiller introduced his successor into the circle of the painter, Wilhelm von Schadow, who was director of the Academy of Fine Arts and occupied a central place in the Art Society known as the *Malkasten*. Schumann joined this society, whose other members included the painters Carl Sohn, Theodor Hildebrandt and Carl Friedrich Lessing, who were all soon attending Schumann's little 'singing circles'. Through the Music Society Schumann met Euler, a lawyer, and Richard Hasenclever and Wolfgang Müller, who were both doctors, the latter also wrote for the *Neue Zeitschrift*. Amongst the musicians, Schumann most often met Wilhelm von Wasielewski, a former pupil at the Leipzig

Conservatory and now leading the orchestra in Düsseldorf (he would later write a biography of Schumann). Clara often played trios with Wasielewski and the cellist Forberg. The young Julius Tausch had also studied at the Leipzig Conservatory. He was now conducting the 'Liedertafel' in Düsseldorf, he occasionally performed as a pianist, gave trio soirées and was also a competent conductor – 'if only the man were personally more pleasant' Clara wrote in her diary (L2,225). Schumann now thoroughly enjoyed the high regard in which he was generally held, his secure position and the 'enthusiasm' of his audiences (L2,229) – he had been deprived of all these for such a long time. The character of the Rhinelanders was infectious – it was many years since he had written in his diary *enthused*, as he did in January 1851 (T3,550). Clara was taken with the 'cheerful unforced behaviour of the ladies', although she added that in her opinion 'there are times when they overstep the bounds of femininity and good taste' (L2,228).

Schumann was composing all the time. A new work was finished almost every month, including the Cello Concerto, Op 129, written in a mere two weeks. He had completed the Rhenish Symphony, Op 97, in a month, on 9 December 1850.

The signal-like character of the fourth, sometimes extended to the seventh or octave, is characteristic of the opening, and drives the whole symphony forward with repeated fanfares for the brass. The same interval characterises the themes of each movement except the third. The opening movement explores the idea of upswing from the early piano pieces. The first theme sets its own rhythmical drive pulse against the regular beat more assertively than in any of Schumann's other symphonies. This, and the broad harmonies with their wide intervals, demonstrates a freedom, also to be found in the dance-like auxiliary theme, a variation on the main theme,[81] and in the iambic theme of the coda. The emphatic climax of the development section is reached when the horns play the theme as a festive fanfare with long note values. In the two following movements the perspective is narrowed to the particular: first the experienced moment and then the remembered moment. The Scherzo, a 'Ländler' in C major, is in remarkable contrast to the wild and bizarre scherzi that Schumann wrote elsewhere, and is reminiscent of the third movement of Beethoven's Pastoral Symphony. In the two trio-like sections the character of the triadic, folksong-like melody (build on triads) is changing. After a comic masquerade, a game with baroques figures behind which the Ländler lurks, the dark side of Florestan's humour is demonstrated in the archaism of the A minor trio, where the dance scene is put into the perspective of the transitoriness of life. This free fantasy with its three themes is followed by a *festive* movement in E flat minor strictly composed with one theme and only based on a structure of fourth in an almost abstract manner. The five rising fourths not only balance the five descending fourths in the main theme of the opening movement (bars 5-13), but the variant of the Ländler theme (II, bar 17) is repeated in the melody, here shortened into quavers (IV bars 6 f). There is a timeless quality to this movement, where the three different measures of the theme, each increasing in length, seem outside real time. The marking of *festive*, often used by Schumann in his later years, the organ-like tone-colours – three trombones give weight to the brass – and the severe polyphony, all suggest sacred music, as does the title he originally gave to it *In the style of an accompaniment to a festive ceremony*, such a ceremony as Schumann witnessed in Cologne Cathedral on 12 November 1850 when Archbishop Geissel was elevated to cardinal. In the sacred, that has been secularised, survived what Schumann missed: continuity, measure, order and the idea of community were all features that Schumann thought he saw in the Catholicism of the Rhineland. He used a similar structure of fourths in the Credo of his Mass (bar 1, 2.Vl). The polyphony in the coda of the finale, and its use of trombones, refers back to the fourth movement; the *festive* theme, now in a bright major key, returns in the exuberant finale, and is linked to the dynamic opening of the symphony by the abundance of its themes and motifs. It reaches its climax towards the end of the development section, but unlike the Second Symphony, Op 61, quotes the tradition – here it is with a new fanfare-like theme in B major, a utopian moment, related in key and substance to the Revolutionary Marches, Op 76 (No 4, bar 36). His use of the third and the sixth refers back to the opening of the symphony, giving the idea of upswing its own momentum.

It is clear how much this symphony meant to Schumann from the references it contains to his earlier symphonic work: a motif from the second movement of the Spring Symphony is quoted in the first movement here (bars 449 ff); the finale contains quotations from the main theme of the introduction to the Second Symphony in C major (bars 556 ff), as well as the fugato theme from the finale of the Fourth Symphony in D minor (bars 303 ff). The way in which music with popular appeal is combined with the artificial is reminiscent of the ideals of the League of David, whose aim was to create a new poetic age through the use of a music that could be generally understood – Schumann intended to pursue this idea, and immediately embarked on an oratorio with Luther as its subject, a work that would be *absolutely in the popular idiom, one that a farmer and a bourgeois could understand* (NF344).

Schumann was contemplating an oratorio, as well as an opera, as can be seen from various overtures composed at this time. In the autumn of 1851 he wrote numerous songs and ballads, a trio, and two violin sonatas that he played through immediately with Wasielewski.

Schumann's position was about to change. A highly critical review of the eighth concert in the subscription series, in March 1851, at which only works by Schumann had been played, set off a discussion on the shortcomings of the concerts. The choir reacted with reluctance to Schumann's weakness as a conductor, his silence, and to the difficult repertoire they were to sing – members arrived late for rehearsals or even missed them altogether. Clara complained bitterly about their lack of respect, their 'gossiping and laughter that often meant that the conductor's voice could hardly be heard'. 'The ladies hardly open their mouths', she wrote, 'they sit to sing and fidget with their hands and feet' (L2,235, 241). *Loneliness*, Schumann noted in his diary. He *wondered* whether to stay in Düsseldorf (T3, 556), but Clara was pregnant once again – their daughter Eugenie was born on 1 December 1851 – so with six children to support, they could not afford for him to give up a secure position. Schumann's short temper now sometimes spilled over into dissatisfaction with his wife's piano playing – she had to put up with 'the most bitter and disheartening accusations' (L2,254). There were diversions from these continual *annoyances* in a visit to Hiller in Cologne, in summer days in *the garden* (T3,557,566), in excursions with the children to the Eller forest, the heathland at Bilk, the Hofgarten or the Benrath Palace, then in July they spent a holiday in the south – according to Clara the 'most beautiful' they had ever had (L2,261). Their boat journey up the Rhine reminded Schumann of his student days; in Heidelberg he found everything just as it had been 22 years before – the landscape, the old houses, the wine. In Chamonix they saw an *eclipse of the sun against Mont Blanc*; Schumann was still marvelling at the *heavenly sights* when they reached home on 5 August 1851 (NF346). In March of the following year they travelled to Leipzig for the last time, for a concert in the Gewandhaus, where the *Manfred Overture*, (the 'most magnificent' of Schumann's works (L2,267) according to Moscheles), the *Pilgrimage of the Rose* and the *Rhenish Symphony* were all performed. Clara rehearsed Schumann's new chamber music with David, Rietz and Grabau, and as Liszt and Joachim had come from Weimar, there was so much music-making that they were afraid 'they would almost be killed by music' (L2,268).

It could no longer be concealed that Schumann was incapable of performing his professional duties. At the first meeting where the winter concerts for 1851 were discussed, complaints were voiced about the way Schumann was managing the choir and the orchestra, and Schumann was once again fearful for the future. He sometimes had difficulty following fast tempi, and from time to time a *strange weakness in his voice* could be noticed (T3,634); later he suffered from acoustical illusions, rather like a sort of tinnitus. The tempi of his works in the last three years of his active composition are almost exclusively moderate or slow. In the first half of 1852 he composed his only two sacred works, a mass and a requiem. Schumann almost always wore black at this time, and he looked rather like a clergyman. Portraits that were made even before this show how he was changing – his pose is strained, almost defensive, and there is a mask-like rigidity in his facial expression. When he fell ill, in April 1852, he thought at first that he was suffering from rheumatism, though later he spoke of a *nervous disorder*, that might be alleviated by bathing in the Rhine. This *period of great suffering* lasted until the end of the year (T3,597, 601), so Tausch was obliged to take the rehearsals for the winter concerts. Schumann now collected together all his early essays and reviews as if his life's work was complete. After searching persistently he finally found a publisher for his *Gesammelte Schriften* (Collected Writing), that should serve as his *memorial* (NF 474). In July Clara realised that she was pregnant once again. They went on holiday in August to Scheveningen, where she suffered a miscarriage. Schumann took the waters, but they brought him no relief. Tausch had to conduct the first two concerts of the season, and when Schumann was able to return to the podium for the first time, in December, the audience was almost hostile. Shortly after this several men on the committee of the Choral Society wrote to Schumann demanding his resignation. Euler and Hasenclever intervened, but even a formal apology from the men concerned was insufficient to make good this humiliation. *Thoughts* about *moving away* went through Schumann's head (T3,611) and even Clara would have most liked to be 'immediately up and away' with him, were it not for the children. She expressed her passionate solidarity with her husband in her diary – her indignation at such 'despicable people', accusing Tausch of weaving intrigues, and seeing 'beastliness' at the heart of it all (L2,245).

At Whitsun Düsseldorf held the Lower Rhine Music Festival,

Robert Schumann portrait 1840

lasting three days. The high point was the performance of Beethoven's Ninth Symphony under Hiller. With great effort Schumann managed to conduct Handel's *Messiah*, and a performance of his own revised Symphony in D minor. This was received *enthusiastically* (T3,625), in contrast to the reception for his Festival Overture on the *Rheinweinlied*.

At the end of July, when on a visit to Bonn, Schumann had

Robert Schumann portrait 1851

his most serious breakdown, described in his diary as an attack of *rheumatism* (T3,631). The doctor who attended him, on the other hand, was of the opinion that Schumann had 'an incurable brain disease' and that he was 'a doomed man' (E2,201). In April Schumann had suddenly begun table-rapping. According to his daughter Eugenie, at that time 'people high and low' were all 'rapping'.[82] Schumann's strange and intense fascination with this craze lasted until the end of the year. Unlike other people, he found a method in this social game of losing himself, escaping from the never-ending hurt and humiliation of his misfortunes. He always referred to these laconically in his diary as the *impertinence* of this or that gentlemen of the Music Society. He protected himself from the meanness of the world[83] with intensive reading, mostly in the evenings, with ordering and collecting his manuscripts, with correcting and other manual work, such as preparing piano reductions or harmonising Bach's violin and cello sonatas. He was often successful, at least for a time, as can be seen from his emphatic and repeated comments *content, busy, happy*. Maybe Clara was taken in by her husband's cheerful demeanour, maybe she was just assisting him in his attempts to escape his fears at the loss of his strength. She suspected that the cause of his medical symptoms was a 'brain disease', yet she wrote in the diary after celebrating her thirty-fourth birthday: 'Am I not the happiest woman on this earth?' (L2,277) She was composing again – for his birthday she had presented her husband with a set of variations on one of his own themes, in June she set six songs from *Jucunde* by Rollett, then in July she wrote Romances for piano and for violin and piano (Op 20, 21, 22). Schumann, on the other hand, at forty-three made an index of his works as if he were writing his last will and testament, in the knowledge that his oeuvre was now complete.

At the end of August Joachim came to visit and played

Schumann's new violin compositions *wonderfully* and *captivating* (T3,634). His friendship with Joachim dated from the music festival in May where he had performed Beethoven's Violin Concerto in such a way that Clara thought she had 'never heard such violin playing' (L2,278). It was Joachim who recommended Johannes Brahms, aged 20, to introduce himself to Schumann. Marie Schumann tells of the 'cheerful young visitor one morning',

Clara Schumann aged 34. Photograph by Franz Hanfstaengl

a 'very young, devastatingly handsome young man with long fair hair' who appeared at the door one day in September.[84] He had brought a folder full of his compositions – sonatas, scherzi, Hungarian folk songs, chamber music, Lieder. He came almost every day, played the piano *especially beautifully* (T3,638), and stayed in Düsseldorf for the whole of October. Schumann was convinced that Brahms would cause *the greatest stir in the musical world*, and at the beginning of November he tried to persuade Härtel to publish Brahms' works, commending them particularly for their *completely original sound effects* (NF484, 486). On 14 October Schumann had written an article[85] for the *Neue Zeitschrift*, his first for ten years, in which he hailed Brahms as *the prophet ideally suited to express the spirit of his time* (GS2,301). Schumann could see that Brahms was making *new tracks,* that were no longer his own. But some of the glory would still be reflected at the end of his road. He saw Brahms as an *eagle*, on the *ascent* (NF 379, 380), and Schumann was able to *calm the wild beating of his wings* before *his first flight above the earth* (NF380,381). His association with the young men, Brahms, Joachim and Albert Dietrich reminded Schumann of the effusive friendships of his youth. These happy October days generated the *idea for a sonata for Joachim* (T3,639), the 'FAE Sonata' for violin and piano, so named for Joachim's motto *frei aber einsam* (free but alone). Dietrich composed the first movement, Schumann the second and fourth, Brahms the third, signing it 'Johannes Kreisler junior'.

Schumann's last orchestral work, his violin concerto, completed in two weeks on 3 October 1853, is quite against the traditional virtuoso concerto. There is no introduction, no solo cadenza, no brilliance. The dark key of D minor is reflected in the tone colours and the deep register of the solo instrument. Extreme economy is the chief principle of his composition: the themes for all the movements are developed from just three melodic elements.[86] The soloist no longer dominates, as he had in the Cello Concerto, Op 129. The Violin Concerto differs from the Piano Concerto, Op 54, or the Cello Concerto in the separation between the expositions for tutti and soloist, and in the harsh way in which the solo instrument and the orchestra oppose each other, almost making them irreconcilable. This mirrors the isolation of the individual in society, as Schumann himself had experienced lately in a threatening way! The 'baroque' main theme of the orchestral exposition, with its tremoli strings and its drum rolls and beats, makes an irrevocable judgement; there is an aura of 'tremendum' introduced by elements of sacred music, while the main theme, which appears three times, also contributes to this. A poetic second subject in F major, a subdued song with a rocking melody resembling a cradle song, is set for a moment against the dominating main theme, an image of the warmth and security for which was so longed for. The solo violin grapples strenuously with the main theme in technically difficult semi-quaver sequences; a similar exertion is also required in the double-stops of the second subject (bar 115ff). The main theme brightens into F major, the key of the second subject. A dream-like longing is expressed in a new theme towards the end of the exposition, as the violin begins a dialogue

Joseph Joachim. Lithograph by E. Kühnel, 1863

with the clarinet and the oboe (dolce, bar 183ff). The D major coda that follows the recapitulation of the main theme in the major key offers the hope of reconciliation – in the harmonic relationship between the second subject, introduced by the violas then paraphrased by the solo violin, and the main theme, now reduced to two bars, without menace or rigidity. The slow movement opens with an ethereal syncopated theme on the cellos, picking up the mood of the rocking cradle-song from the second subject that immediately precedes it, while the octaves in the background slightly recall the ponderous opening of the first movement. The violin, with its song-like theme, begins a dialogue with the cello theme, an exchange between orchestra and soloist (bar 13ff) that can be seen as a visualisation of a different society, one in which the individual could find his place. However, the sudden hesitations of the dark middle section bring back the inner emotion of the first movement, so the reprise of the solo theme comes in the relative minor key. At the end of this movement an octave motif for the violin can be heard as counterpoint to the syncopated theme, developing into an extended opening for the finale in D major, a sonata rondo where the theme of the refrain reintroduces the leaps of octaves and sixths from the first movement. A polonaise – a stalking dance with which society reflects itself – becomes the stage for free interaction, when all voices play together. The dialogue of the middle movement is continued in the playful exchange between a scherzo-like woodwind motif and the cantilena of the solo violin, and this time it is the solo instrument that introduces the new variations out of the couplets; there is a contrast with the first movement in the expansiveness of the intervals and in their higher register. A 'closing song' is created in the combination of solo passages and a singing horn melody. Maybe it was this finale that encouraged Schumann to offer this work to his publisher as *a thoroughly cheerful piece* (NF485).

Joseph Joachim, for whom the concerto was written, only played it through, finding it 'incredibly difficult, particularly the last movement'.[87] After Schumann's death Joachim, Brahms, and even Clara Schumann herself, all wondered if it was worthy of publication. The work was only printed in 1937 and had its first performance in Berlin that same year.

Schumann composed his last work for piano in October, the *Gesänge der Frühe*

Johannes Brahms. Drawing by J J B Laurent, 1853. Brahms at 20 looked as young as this when he first met Clara and Robert Schumann.

(Songs of Dawn). The original dedication had been *An Diotima*, and the coded references to the names Diotima (D-A) and Hyperion (H-E) remain in the opening notes.[88] The songs of this cycle are five pieces with a strophic structure, including a chorale, a duet and a hunting song. The archaic sound of the first and last pieces, the plagal cadences and the strange harmonies alienated with single dissonant notes are all reminiscent of Hölderlin's odes and elegies to 'Diotima', with their antique verse forms. There are links throughout the cycle in the progression of keys, and particularly in the recurring motifs and groups of intervals (the fifths of the opening).[89] 'Dawn' signifies the *new tracks*, the *Neue Bahnen* of which Schumann had written in his article that same October. The musical expression of this new beginning is provided by the unison sequence of perfect fifths in the first piece, played three times. The horn calls of the central piece, whose fanfares lead to new harmonic vistas through modulation into mediant keys, are reminders of 'Upswing' (Op 12 No 2) and the bright hopes of early years. The metaphor of dawn is itself ambiguous. 'As in days of old' the 'voices' sing in Hölderlin's ode *Der Abschied* (Farewell). Schumann's *Gesänge* also points to the *Dawn* of the past. The last piece sounds like an old melody transferred to an even earlier period by a sort of chorale prelude and figurative variation. Its solemn tone, the calm measure of the music and lack of syncopative tension, all point to the image of 'reconciliation' as at the end of Hyperion: where 'Everything that is separated shall be reunited'. As Schumann looks back, in farewell, there are memories: of folk songs of the second and the fourth pieces, of Kreisleriana, Op 16 No 6, in the last piece, of the early Nocturne in F sharp minor, No 4, while the leaping motif of bars 25/26 and the arpeggios at the end are reminiscent of the introduction to the Sonata in F sharp minor, Op 11. The diminuendo endings of these pieces themselves speak of farewell: the restraint of the first piece, the way the second sinks into a coda, and then the end of the group, gradually fading away.

On 7 November Schumann learned the decision of the committee – the men spoke with his wife, not with him – Tausch would take over direction of the chorus and the orchestra. Schumann might only conduct his own works, if he so wished. He tried to follow the proper procedures, insisted on the terms of his *contract* and gave his notice as of October 1854, although he did not conduct again. *Tired of these vulgar events* Robert and Clara wanted to *leave* Düsseldorf *completely* (NF383), and once again Vienna seemed their best hope.

Schumann composed nothing more after the day on which he was 'given notice'; only the simple piano accompaniments to Paganini's Caprices appeared in 1855. A concert tour to Holland at the end of the year afforded some relief. Robert and Clara both thought of this tour as a triumph. There were performances of the Second and Third Symphonies, the Piano Concerto, the *Concert Allegro*, Op 134, the Quintet and the *Pilgrimage of the Rose*. Schumann noted *honours even for me – unexpected* (T2,441). Even the question from a Dutch prince to Clara Schumann during a soirée at court, as to whether Robert Schumann was also musical and which instrument he played, could hardly spoil their good mood. In January Schumann began to put together writings on music that he found in world literature: his *Dichtergarten* (Poet's Garden). In the middle of the month there was a reunion with Brahms and Joachim in Hanover with many hours spent making music together, and performances of the Fourth Symphony and the Violin Fantasy, Op 131.

The diary entries up to 17 February tell of his last *period of suffering*, beginning with a *painful ear disorder* on 10 February 1854 (T3,648). The pages are empty after that, except for notes of a few expenses. Schumann was hearing in his head not just one note but symphonic music, that he found *wonderful* at first – he wrote down one of the themes he heard [90] – but this soon became hellish noises so that 'he cried out in pain' (L2,297). He no longer felt himself, and was overcome with fears for his own predictability, the humiliations of his life made him aggressive. He saw himself as an 'evil person' who might do harm to his wife (L2,298f), so on 26 February he made the decision to enter a psychiatric clinic. He put together the papers and other things he wished to take with him. Then the next day he jumped from the bridge into the Rhine. He was pulled out and a few days later was taken to the sanatorium run by Dr Richarz in Endenich, near Bonn.

Clara Schumann was helped at this difficult time by Brahms, Joachim and Dietrich. Paul Mendelssohn, brother of the composer, assisted with a loan of 400 talers while the publisher Härtel offered a benefit concert. Schumann's position as Director

The Old Ships Bridge in Düsseldorf. Steel engraving by Emil Höfer (1845) after a drawing by Dielmann

of Music was not filled immediately, and his salary continued to be paid. Schumann was visited from time to time by his young friends Brahms, Joachim, Dietrich, Grimm, Wasielewski, and also Ms Bargiel and Hasenclever. The doctors advised Clara against a meeting with her husband, so she never went to visit him – she did not want to bear 'to see him like this' (L2,323).

In Endenich Schumann retreated more and more into the ancient past, reading Homer and Plato for his *Dichtergarten*. From time to time he suffered from acoustical hallucinations to his hearing and manifestations of insanity, then at other times the doctor found him 'gentle, friendly and cheerful'.[91] *The music was now silent* (NF392). In September he asked for the first time about his family. He replied to news from his wife, as she wrote, 'so gently, so lovingly' (L2,330); he reminded her of the letters that he had sent her to Paris 15 years before, and wrote of his longing: *If only I could see you just once and speak to you, but it is too far*. His years with Clara seemed like *a dream: blessed times from the past* (NF397, 399). When he learned of the birth of his son on 11

June 1854 he decided on the name of Felix, in memory of Mendelssohn. During the first year in Endenich he was able to play the piano a little on good days, and to read compositions by Brahms. He wrote letters, in very legible handwriting, to his friends, to his publisher and also to his children, after whom he constantly asked. He had books sent, including his *Gesammelte Schriften* that had been printed by Wigand, he read the *Flegeljahre* once again and walked happily as far as the Beethoven memorial in Bonn. Then his situation worsened. He now had hallucinations and panic attacks about things from which he had suffered during his life – he had a fear of being poisoned, of the Nemesis.[92] He felt helplessly in its clutches, screamed aloud, had outbursts of anger and became violent with his attendants. At the beginning of 1855 he wrote to his wife: *How sad if I should not see you and the children ever again!* (L2,364) He was visited in May by Bettina von Arnim who reported on his homesickness, on his attempts 'to control himself' (L2,376) and also on how difficult it had become for him to speak; she did not believe, however, that Schumann was so ill that he needed to remain in the institution. Wasielewski on the other hand found him completely 'broken' (W497), and Joachim wrote to Hanslick about his last visit to Endenich that Schumann had leafed through his old compositions 'with feverish excitement' and 'played them with stumbling hands on the keyboard' (Q193). In his last communication, of 5 May 1855, Schumann started a letter to his wife with the sentence: *There is a shadow hovering*; and for the last time he named the people who were dearest to him: Clara, Brahms and Mendelssohn (L2,374).

Clara had resumed her concert tours in October 1854. The clinic was expensive, the accommodation costs alone coming to 50 talers a month. At the beginning of 1856 she went to Vienna, then to England for three months. The company of Brahms, with his 'gentle sympathy that does me so much good' and his high

The Schumann children: from left to right, Ludwig, Marie, Felix, Elise (standing at the back), Ferdinand and Eugenie. Photograph, circa 1855. Their daughter Julie is missing.

spirits, helped her endure her unhappiness. They wrote to one another when she was on tour, and each 'wished the other was there' (L2,317, 346).

In April 1856 Clara heard from Dr Richarz that her husband was 'ill beyond help' (L2,412). The signs of progressive paralysis, probably a consequence of neurosyphilis, were becoming increasingly evident. He was making imaginary journeys with an atlas, writing down the names of cities and countries in alphabetical order. His speech had become 'almost unintelligible'.[93] Clara saw him again on 27 July after the doctor had telegraphed. Schumann was very thin, he had been refusing to eat for weeks, and only taking a little wine and jelly; it is not known if he recognised his wife. He died on 29 July, at four in the afternoon. There was no one with him. He was buried in the evening of 31 July in the cemetery at Bonn. There were only few to accompany his coffin: Clara Schumann, Brahms, Joachim and Hiller. Then suddenly, reported Klaus Groth, the cemetery was 'dark with people' as they came from all the streets around, 'as if there had been news of a great disaster' (E2,229).

Clara Schumann survived her husband by forty years. She was buried at his side.

Robert Schumann's gravestone in Bonn. Designed by Adolf Donndorf, 1879–1880. Clara sits admiringly at the feet of her husband

Notes:

1   Emil Flechsig: 'Erinnerungen an Robert Schumann' in *Neue Zetischrift für Musik*, 117, 1956, vol 7/8, p 392.

2   Ibid.

3   Ibid.

4   In the curriculum vitae which he submitted to the University of Jena in 1840 (Q 15)

5   *Fantasiestücke in Callots Manier* in Collected works, vol 1, (Frankfurt am Main, 1967), p 31.

6   Flechsig: Erinnerungen, p 393.

7   Several sections of the diary bear the title Lebensschnecke (T1,75 ff). Cf the descriptions Trödelschnecke and Notenschnecke in Jean Paul's *Flegeljahren*.

8   Abbreviated version in Frauke Otto: Robert Schumann als Jean Paul-Leser (Frankfurt am Main, 1984), pp 25-43.

9   Karl Immermann: Die Epigonen. Familienmemoiren in neun Büchern. Ed Benno von Wiese (Frankfurt am Main, 1971), p 122.

10 Mauricio Kagel, who set Schumann's Selene fragments to music in 1986, thought that Arnold Schönberg might have wished just such a text for Pierrot lunaire.

11 Immermann: Die Epigonen, p 120.

12 Abridged in Otto: Robert Schumann, pp 109–114.

13 Reproduced in Otto: Robert Schumann, pp 66–75.

14 Friedrich Täglichsbeck, quoted in Wilhelm Josef von Wasielewski: Schumanniana (Bonn, 1883). p 91.

15 Diary 1 refers to Gretchen am Spinnrad (153), Erlkönig, Das Heimweh, Die Allmacht and Wanderers Nachtlied (156).

16 Flechsig: Erinnerungen, p 393.

17 Ibid.

18 1834, in a letter to Freiherr von Fricken, quoted in Wolfgang Boetticher: Robert Schumanns Klavierwerke. Neue biographische

und textkritische Untersuchungen. Part 2, (Wilhelmshaven, 1984), p 49.

19 Flechsig: Erinnerungen, p 394.

20 The variations are no longer existent.

21 Eugenie Schumann: Robert Schumann. Ein Lebensbild meines Vaters (Leipzig, 1931), p 127.

22 Schumann later showed, using Schubert as an example, *how new art created its own Palestrina songs* (GS2,337).

23 The name belonged to an acquaintance, Meta Abegg, and also to a student mentioned in his diary.

24 Adolph Kohut: Friedrich Wieck. Ein Lebens-und Künstlerbild. (Dresden, Leipzig 1888), p 73.

25 Probably a quotation from E T A Hoffmann's Serapionsbrüder. Complete works, vol. 2, (Frankfurt am Main, 1967), p 373.

26 More recently Wolfgang Boetticher and Jacques Chailley.

27 Reinhart Koselleck: Vergange Zukunft. Zur Semantik geschichtlicher Zeiten. (Frankfurt am Main, 1979), p 329.

28 Ibid. p 330.

29 Heinrich Heine: Lutetia II. In Collected Works, vol 4. (Munich 1972), p 324.

30 Sergei Prokofiev: Dokumente, Briefe, Erinnerungen, (Leipzig 1965), p 137.

31 'Robert Schumanns letzte Lebensjahre. Protokoll einer Krankheit'. In Archiv-Blätter 1 der Akademie der Künste, (Berlin 1994), p 21.

32 *Allgemeine Musikalische Zeitung*, Nr. 49, p 806.

33 This use of pseudonyms started with the Tunnel über der Pleisse. See Bernhard Appel: 'Schumanns Davidsbund. Geistes- und sozialgeschichtliche Voraussetzungen einer romantischen Idee', in Archiv für Musikwissenschaft, 37, 1981, vol 1, p 15.

34 Collected works, vol 1, p 20, Ed Norbert Miller, (Frankfurt am Main, 1960).

35 Although many of his friends were members of the Leipzig 'Tunnel' (Brendel, Dorn, Herlosssohn, von der Lühe, Lyser, Marschner, Stegmayer, Wieck) Schumann himself disliked clubs.

36 Des Vetters Eckfenster (1822). Richard Sennett who quotes this example, charts the development of the silent observer in the 19th century (Verfall und Ende des öffentlichen Lebens.

Die Tyrannei der Intimität). (Frankfurt am Main, 1983), p 225 f)

37 Encouragement came from Ernst Ortlepp.

38 The network of correspondents established by Schumann was unusual for a music journal at this time.

39 *I may not speak about the following Papillons etc because of the blood-relationship of the composer with this journal.* (E2,245)

40 Friedrich Schlegel wrote that 'poetry can only be criticised in poetry', Lyceums-Fragment No 117. (Kritische Friedrich-Schlegel-Ausgabe, Ed. Ernst Behler, vol 2, part 1, Munich/Paderborn/Vienna, 1967, p 162). Schumann found an example for his poetic criticism in E T A Hoffmann.

41 *Both kinds, that is, dissection of the mechanical and poetic description had their advantages, the latter in its lack of dryness.* (GS1,423)

42 Karl Laux: Robert Schumann, (Leipzig 1982), p 45.

43 The *Préambule* was originally intended for the opening of the variations on Schubert's Sehnsuchtswalzer.

44 He first appears in the German title as the author (Fasching. Schwänke auf vier Noten f. Pfte. von Florestan); Schumann agreed to the French title at the request of his publisher.

45 Die Serapions-Brüder. In: Collected Works, vol 2, (Frankfurt am Main, 1967), p 352 ff.

46 Jean Paul: 'Des Luftschiffers Giannozzo Seebuch. Komischer Anhang zum Titan'. In Collected Works, ed Norbert Miller, vol 3. (Munich/Vienna, 1961), p 942.

47 August Göllerich: Franz Liszt (Berlin, 1908), p 45.

48 E T A Hoffmann: Kreisleriana. In Collected Works. vol I. (Frankfurt am Main, 1967), p 245.

49 E T A Hoffmann: Lebensansichten des Katers Murr. In Collected Works, vol 3, p 248.

50 Ernst Bloch: Das Prinzip Hoffnung. (Frankfurt am Main, 1959), p 1628.

51 Willi Reich: Alban Berg. (Munich, Zurich 1985), pp 194–206.

52 *Sent the Sarazin to Liszt* (T2,54); *Sarazin and Suleika* (T2,477). See Alfred Cortot: Vorwort zu den Novelletten. (Paris, New York, 1947)

53 Line 7 in the poem transcribed by Schumann 'As with the most fervent contentment' from the *Buch der Suleika.*

54 During work on his Op 21 Schumann noted *fugues and canons in all my fantasising* (T2,53).

55 These quotations are from the legal documents of the Dresden State Archive, analysed by Hans John and reproduced in part in: Schumann-Studien 1 (Zwickau, 1988), pp 38-46.

56 They were originally in a different order: 3, 1, 5, 2, 6, 8, 9, 12, 4, 10, 11, 7.

57 At this point (as if they were fleeing home), instead of the tonic triad of the sixth chord of the dominant fifth, the subdominant, whose resolution extends into the coda

58 Bach polyphony is used here in an almost modern way: the dissonances, the bold leading of the singing voice, the almost spoken ending appear in a similar way in Schönberg's George songs.

59 Originally there were 20. The superfluous songs were published as Op 127 Nos 2 and 3 and Op 142 Nos 2 and 4.

60 This appeared later as Robert Schumann's Op 37 and Clara Schumann's Op 12.

61 The model for the link between introduction and exposition was Schubert's C major Symphony.

62 Jean Paul: Flegeljahre. In Collected Works, Ed Norbert Miller. vol 1/2, (Munich and Vienna, 1959), p 771.

63 From Op 16 No 6 in the larghetto, bars 9ff, from Op 16 No 8 in the finale, bars 43ff.

64 Schumann: Erinnerungen an Felix Mendelssohn Barthody. (Published by the Städtischen Museum Zwickau, Ed Georg Eismann, Zwickau 1947), p 13.

65 They have been cited as a reference to the aria 'Es ist vollbracht' from Bach's St John Passion (Hans Kohlhase: Die Kammermusik Robert Schumanns. Stilistische Untersuchungen. vol 2I, Hamburg 1979, p 85).

66 Richard Wagner: Collected Letters. Ed Gertrud Ströbel and Werner Wolf, vol. 2. (Leipzig, 1970). p 326.

67 Jenseits von Gut und Böse. S Hauptstück, No 245. In Collected works, Critical Edition, ed Giorgio Colli and Mazzino Montinari. vol 2, part 6, p 196.

68 Paula and Walter Rehberg: Robert Schumann. Sein Leben und sein Werk. (Stuttgart, 1954) p 700, note 140.

69 *Allgemeine Musikalische Zeitung*, December 1843, p 952; January 1844, p 28.

70 Felix Mendelssohn Bartholdy: Briefe aus Leipziger Archiven. Ed, Hans-Joachim Rothe and Reinhard Szeskus (Leipzig, 1972) Intro. p 10-11.

71 Ibid. p 11.

72 Heinrich Laube: Reisenovellen, vol 3 (Leipzig, 1908), p 126.

73 Richard Wanger: Sämtliche Briefe, vol 2, p 216.

74 E T A Hoffmann: Collected Works, vol 1, p 245.

75 They were Carl Ritter and Heinrich Richter, son of the artist Ludwig Richter.

76 Schumann was not yet aware of the reconciliation in the 'epilogue'.

77 Friedrich Hebbel: Sämtliche Werke. Historisch-kritische Ausgabe. Ed. Richard Maria Werner. Part 2, Tagebücher, vol 1 (Berlin, 1905), p 319.

78 In 1993 *Manfred* was staged as a co-production in the opera houses of Lyon, Strassburg and Brussels (in German).

79 These hitherto unpublished pieces were edited by Jörg Demus, Milan 1978.

80 Manfred, Act 1, final scene.

81 The leaps of fourths and sixths at the beginning are repeated in the second movement, bars 103-106.

82 Eugenie Schumann: Robert Schumann, p 380.

83 Letter to Robert Franz. In Briefe und Dokumente im Schumannhaus Bonn-Endenich, Ed Thomas Synofzik (Bonn, 1993), p 32.

84 Eugenie Schumann: Robert Schumann, p 357.

85 Schumann withdrew this article from his Gesammelte Schriften on account of the weak reaction to it.

86 From the leaps of octaves and sixths, from the arching motif in the secondary subject of the first movement, and from the alternating note motif (1st movt bar 71; 2nd movt syncopated theme; 3rd movt staccato motif, bar 68)

87 Johannes Joachim and Andreas Moser (Ed): Briefe von und an Joseph Joachim. vol 1, (Berlin, 1911), p 453.

88 See Michael Struck: 'Literarischer Eindruck, poetischer Ausdruck und Struktur in Robert Schumanns Instrumentalmusik'. In:

Robert Schumann und die Dichter. Publ. by the Heinrich-Heine-Institute. Ed Joseph A. Kruse (Düsseldorf, 1991), p 120.

89   Individually examined in Michael Struck: Die unstrittenen späten Instrumentalwerke Schumanns (Hamburg, 1984), p 477 ff.

90   The theme in E flat major, on which he wrote variations a few days later, the so-called Ghost Variations, corresponding to the opening of the solo theme in the second movement of the Violin Concerto (bar 5). Brahms also wrote variations on the theme (Op 23).

91   Archiv-Blätter I, p 17 (See footnote 31).

92   Ibid, p 18.

93   Ibid. p 22.

Chronology

Year	Age	Life
1810		Robert Schumann is born on 8 June in Zwickau.
1817	7	Starts to study the piano.
1819	9	Clara Wieck is born on 13 September in Leipzig.
1820	10	Pupil of the Lyceum in Zwickau
1822	12	Psalm 150, piece for piano performed in concerts in the school
1825	15	Death of his sister Emilie
1826	16	Death of his father
1827	17	First compositions of songs. Starts writing a diary. Reads Jean Paul. Gets to know the music of Schubert.
1828	18	*Juniusabende und Julytage. Die Tonwelt. Selene.* High school exams. Travels to Bayreuth and Munich. Meets Heine. Starts to study law in Leipzig. Studies the piano with Friedrich Wieck. Clara Wieck's first concert in the Gewandhaus in Leipzig.
1829	19	Two semesters in Heidelberg. Travels to Italy
1830	20	*Abegg-Variationen* op. 1. He hears Paganini in Frankfurt. He decides to become a musician. Studies with Wieck and lives in his house.

Year	History	Culture
1810	Karl XIII of Sweden adopts a French general, Johannes Bernadotte, as his heir.	Beethoven, music to Goethe's *Egmont*. Chopin is born.
1817	German students meet on the Wartburg. James Monroe becomes US-president.	Constable, *Flatford Mill*. Byron, *Manfred*. Hegel, *Encyclopedia of Philosophy*
1819	Stamford Raffles founds Singapore. US purchases Florida from Spain.	Schubert, *Trout Quintet*. John Keats, 'Ode to a Nightingale'.
1820	English king George III dies. German socialist Friedrich Engels is born.	Pushkin, *Ruslan and Ludmila*. Scott, *Ivanhoe*. Shelley, *Prometheus*. W. Blake, *Jerusalem*
1822	Greece declares its independence from Turkey. Liberia is founded by freed slaves. Bolivar liberates Ecuador.	Stendhal, *About Love*. Schubert, *Die Unvollendete*
1825	Bolivia under President Bolivar becomes an independent republic; end of Spanish colonial rule in South America.	Jean Paul dies. Pushkin, *Boris Godunov.* Antonio Salieri dies. Beethoven, *Great Fuge in B-Major*
1826	Seku Ahmadu conquers Timbuktu.	James Fenimore Cooper, *Last of the Mohicans*.
1827	English and French navies win the Battle of Navarino against Turkish-Egyptian fleet. Bolivar elected president for life of Peru.	Heine, *Buch der Lieder.* Beethoven dies. Schubert, *Die Winterreise*
1828	Russia declares war on Turkey.	Schubert, C Major Symphony and *Klavierstücke*. Thomas Carlyle's *Essay on Goethe*.
1829	In Britain, Robert Peel founds the Metropolitan Police force.	G Rossini, *William Tell*. Delacroix, *Sardanapalus*.
1830	France invades Algeria. Revolution in Paris. Revolution in Belgium. Revolts in parts of Germany.	Hector Berlioz, *Symphonie Fantastique*. Stendhal, *Le Rouge et le Noir*.

1831	21	*Papillions* op. 2. First newspaper article and first published composition. Tuition in theory with Dorn. Probably infected with syphilis. Clara Wieck goes on a concert tour to Paris.
1832	22	Performance of the Symphony in g-minor in Zwickau. His right middle finger stiffens.
1833	23	Bond of David. Death of his brother Julius. Death of his sister-in-law Rosalie. Depressions. Friendship with Ludwig Schunke. Clara Wieck's op. 3 is published, dedicated to Robert.
1834	24	3 April: first edition of *The New Periodical for Music*. Clara jealous of Ernestine von Fricken, with whom Robert is in love and engaged to.
1835	25	*Carnaval* op. 9. Sonata in fis-minor, op. 11. Ends his connection with Ernestine, and beginning of an intensive friendship with Clara. Mendelssohn becomes director of the Leipzig Gewandhaus concerts.
1836	26	Death of his mother. Visits Clara in Dresden. Wieck forbids further meetings. Separation of Robert and Clara lasting 18 months. Meets Chopin.
1837	27	*Davidsbündlertänze* op. 6. Re-establishes contact with Clara. Wieck refuses his offer of marriage. Clara and Wieck set off for Vienna in the autumn where she has her greatest success. Her Op 8 published.
1838	28	*Kinderszenen* op. 15. *Kreisleriana* op. 16. September to April 1839: stays in Vienna; discovers C-Major Symphony and other manuscripts by Schubert. Intensive secret correspondence with Clara.
1839	29	Death of his brother Eduard. Clara embarks on a concert tour without her father to Paris lasting till August. Wieck refuses to allow their marriage, so Clara and Robert appeal to the court. Clara moves to stay with her mother in Berlin.
1840	30	138 Songs. Honorary doctorate from the University of Jena. Meets Liszt. The court permits the marriage. 12 September marriage in Leipzig.
1841	31	*Frühlingssymphonie* op. 38. First movement of Piano Concerto op. 54. Symphony in d-minor, op. 120 (1st version). Birth of daughter Marie on 1 September.
1842	32	Accompanies Clara on concert tour to north Germany, but returns home while she continues to Copenhagen. Beginning of Robert's nervous illness that recurs with ever-greater frequency.

1831	In Belgium, Leopold of Saxe-Coburg becomes king of independent state. Charles Darwin begins voyage on the Beagle.	Vincenzo Bellini, *Norma*. Victor Hugo, *Notre-Dame de Paris*. Eugène Delacroix, *La Liberté guidant le peuple*.
1832	Britain proclaims sovereignty over Falkland Islands. Turkish-Egyptian War. In Continental Europe, first railway.	Gaetano Donizetti, *L'Elisir d'Amore*. Alexander Pushkin, *Eugene Onegin*. Johann Wolfgang von Goethe, *Faust* (part II).
1833	In British Empire, slavery abolished. Michael Faraday discovers electrolysis.	Felix Mendelssohn, Fourth Symphony.
1834	South Australia Act is passed allowing for establishment of colony there. Civil war in Spain.	James Whistler dies.
1835	'September Laws' in France severely censor the press and suppress the radical movement.	Hans Andersen, *Fairy Tales*. N Gogol, *Dead Souls*. G Donizetti, *Lucy of Lammermoor*.
1836	Texas becomes independent of Mexico. In south Africa, Great Trek of Boers.	R W Emerson's *Nature* founds Transcendentalism.
1837	In Britain, William IV dies; Victoria becomes queen (until 1901). In US, Martin van Buren becomes president. In Canada, rebellions in Upper and Lower Canada (until 1838).	Charles Dickens, *Pickwick Papers*.
1838	In Britain, People's Charter initiates Chartist movement. Steamship services established between Britain and US.	In London, National Gallery opens.
1839	Beginning of Opium War between China and Britain. Britain proclaims New Zealand a colony.	Dickens, *Nicholas Nicelkby*. Edgar Allan Poe, *Tales of the Grotesque and Arabesque*.
1840	In New Zealand, Treaty of Waitangi: Maori chiefs surrender sovereignty to Britain. In Canada, Act of Union joins Lower and Upper Canada.	Adolphe Sax invents the saxophone. P J Proudhon, *Qu'est-ce-que la Propriété?*
1841	Egypt declares independence from Turkey. Second Anglo-Afghan War.	In Britain, *Punch* magazine founded.
1842	France occupies Tahiti, Guinea and Gabon. Britain acquires Hong Kong.	Richard Wagner, *Rienzi*. Alfred Lord Tennyson, *Morte D'Arthur and Other Idylls*.

1843	33	*Das Paradies und die Peri,* op. 50. Meets Berlioz. Lectureship at the conservatory in Leipzig. Birth of daughter Elise on 25 April. Reconciliation between Wieck and Clara and Robert.
1844	34	Joint tour of Russia from February to March. Begins work on *Faust* (finished in 1853). Resigns from the work on the periodical. First breakdown in August. Move from Leipzig to Dresden in December.
1845	35	Birth of daughter Julie on 11 March. First performance of Robert's Piano Concerto in A minor in Dresden with Clara as soloist.
1846	36	Symphony in C-Major, op. 61. Birth of son Emil on 8 February. Recuperates on Norderney. Robert and Clara set off for Vienna in November.
1847	37	Death of Emil in June. Schumann Festival in Zwickau.
1848	38	Opera *Genoveva. Album für die Jugend,* op. 68. Birth of son Ludwig on 20 January.
1849	39	*Manfred* op. 115. Death of his brother Carl. May uprising in Dresden. Clara takes Robert and the children to Maxen, then Kreischa. Birth of son Ferdinand on 16 July.
1850	40	Cello Concerto, op. 129. *Rheinische Sinfonie,* op. 97. Premiere of *Genoveva.* Clara is successful in Hamburg. Family moves to Düsseldorf where Robert becomes music director.
1851	41	First disputes with choir and orchestra. Birth of daughter Eugenie on 1 December.
1852	42	*Messe,* op. 147 and *Requiem,* op. 148. Serious illness. Recuperates in Scheveningen. Increasing conflicts with the concert committee lead to calls for his resignation.
1853	43	Violin Concerto. *Gesänge der Frühe,* op. 133. Beginning of close friendship with Joseph Joachim and Johannes Brahms. Terminates his contract as music director. Successful tour of Holland by Robert and Clara.
1854	44	*Collected Works on Music and Musicians* is published. Work on *Dichtergarten.* Hallucinations. *Geistervariationen.* Attempted suicide on 27 February. He enters the asylum in Endenich on 4 March. Brahms moves to Düsseldorf. Birth of son Felix on 11 June. Clara resumes her concert career.

1843	In India, Britain annexes Sind. In south Africa, Britain proclaims Natal a colony.	Wagner, *Flying Dutchman*. John Stuart Mill, *Logic*.
1844	In Morocco, war with France.	Dumas, *The Count of Monte Cristo*.
1845	In Ireland, potato famine. In India Anglo-Sikh War.	Benjamin Disraeli, *Sybil*.
1846	Mexico-US War (until 1848). In southern Africa, second Xhosa War.	Hector Berlioz, *The Damnation of Faust*. Felix Mendelssohn, *Elijah*.
1847	In Yucután Peninsula, War of the Castes. In France, reform banquets held. In Switzerland, Sonderund War. In California, gold rush begins.	Death of Felix Mendelssohn on 4 November. Charlotte Brontë, *Jane Eyre*. Emily Brontë, *Wuthering Heights*. Giuseppe Verdi, *Macbeth*.
1848	In continental Europe, revolutions in: Sicily; Naples; Paris; Vienna; Venice; Milan; Warsaw; and Cracow.	William Thackeray, *Vanity Fair*. Engels and Marx, *The Communist Manifesto*.
1849	In Rome, republic proclaimed; French troops take Rome.	Dickens, *David Copperfield*.
1850	J W Brett lays first submarine cable, between Dover and Calais.	Nathanial Hawthorne, *The Scarlet Letter*. Honoré de Balzac dies.
1851	In France, Louis Napoleon leads coup d'état. Isaac Singer invents sewing machine.	Herman Melville, *Moby Dick*.
1853	France annexes New Caledonia. Russia conquers Kazakhstan.	Verdi, *Il Trovatore* and *La Traviata*.
1854	In US, Republican Party founded. Pope Pius X declare the dogma of Immaculate Conception of Blessed Virgin Mary to be an article of faith.	Hector Berlioz, *L'enfance du Christ*. *Le Figaro*, Paris, issued.
1855	In Russia, Nicholas I dies; Alexander II becomes tsar. In southern Africa, David Livingstone 'discovers' Victoria Falls.	Robert Browning, *Men and Women*. Gaskell, *North and South*. Walt Whitman, *Leaves of Grass*.

| 1856 | 46 | Clara goes on a concert tour to Vienna, and first tour to England. Visits Robert on 24 July. He dies five days later. He is buried on 31 July in the Old Cemetery, Bonn. Clara writes her last composition, the *Romanze* in B minor. |
| 1896 | | Clara dies on 20 May following second stroke. |

1856	Treaty of Paris: integrity of Turkey is recognized. Second Anglo-Chinese war. Henry Bessemer discovers process of converting iron into steel.	Liszt, *Hungarian Rhapsodies*. Gustave Flaubert, *Madame Bovary*.
1896	Theodore Herzl founds Zionism. First Olympic Games of the modern era held in Athens. Antoine Becquerel discovers radioactivity of uranium.	Puccini, *La Bohème*. Thomas Hardy, *Jude the Obscure*. Nobel Prizes established.

List of Works

Symphonies:

Symphony in g, "Zwickau" (unfinished) 1832

Symphony in c (sketches for 2 movements) 1841

Symphony #1 in Bb, Op. 38, "Spring" 1841

Symphony #2 in C, Op. 62 1845-6

Symphony #3 in Eb, Op. 97, "Rhenish" 1850

Symphony #4 in d, Op. 120 1841, revised 1851

Overtures:

Overture, Scherzo & Finale in E, Op. 52 1840

Overture in c to Schiller's *Bride of Messina*, Op. 100 1850-1

Overture in f to Shakespeare's *Julius Caesar*, Op. 128 1851

Overture in b to Goethe's *Hermann und Dorothea*, Op. 136 1851

Festival Overture on the "Rheinweinlied," Op. 123 (w/chorus) 1853

Work for Solo Instruments or Orchestras:

Piano Concerto in F (unfinished), 1829

Piano Concerto in F (unfinished), 1830

Introduction, theme (Paganini) & sketches for 4 variations in b (pf) 1830

Piano Concerto in D (unfinished) 1833

Piano Concerto in A, Op. 54 1st mvt 1841; 2nd & 3rd mvts 1845

Konzertstück in F, Op. 86 (4 horns) 1849

Konzertstück (Introduction & Allegro appassionato) in G, Op. 92 (pf) 1849

Cello Concerto in A, Op. 129 1850

Fantasy in C, Op. 131 (vn)

Introduction & Allegro in d, Op. 134 (pf) 1853

Violin Concerto in D 1853

Chamber Music:

Piano Quartet in C 1829

Sketches for 2 string quartets (lost) 1839

Trio (material afterwards used in Op. 88) before 1842

String Quartet #1 in a, Op. 41/1 1842

String Quartet #2 in F, Op. 41/2 1842

String Quartet #3 in A, Op. 41/3 1842

Piano Quintet in Eb, Op. 44 1842

Piano Quartet in Eb, Op. 47 1842

Fantasiestücke for pf, vn, vc, Op. 88 1842

Andante & Variations for 2 pfs, 2 vcs, hn [see also Op. 46] 1843

Piano Trio #1 in d, Op. 63 1847

Piano Trio #2 in F, Op. 80 1847

Piano Trio #3 in g, Op. 110 1851

Märchenerzählungen for pf, cl, va, Op. 132 1853

Adagio & Allegro in Ab, Op. 70 (hn, pf) 1849

Fantasiestücke, Op. 73 (cl, pf) 1849

3 Romances, Op. 94 (ob, pf) 1849

5 Stücke im Volkston, Op. 102 (vc, pf) 1849

Märchenbilder, Op. 113 (va, pf) 1849

Violin Sonata #1 in a, Op. 105 1851

Violin Sonata #2 in d, Op. 121 1851

2nd & 4th mvts for "FAE" Sonata (vn, pf) (1st mvt by Dietrich, 3rd mvt by Brahms) 1852

Piano:

"Abegg" Variations, Op. 1 1830

Sonata in Ab (1st mvt & Adagio only) 1830?

Allegro in b, Op. 8 1831

Variations in G on an original theme, "Mit Gott" 1831-2

Prelude & Fugue 1832

Papillons, Op. 2 1832

Études after Paganini's Caprices, Op. 3 1832

6 Intermezzi, Op. 4 1832

Fandango in f# (later used in Op. 11) 1832

Phantasie satyrique, after Henri Herz (unfinished) 1832

Exercise fantastique 1832

Toccata in C, Op. 7 1832

Sketch for a movement in Bb 1832?

Sketch for a fugal piece in bb 1832?

Sketch for a canonic piece in A 1832?

Fugue (probably intended as finale for Op. 5) 1832?

Impromptus on a theme by Clara Wieck, Op. 5 1833

Sehnsuchtswalzervariationen (opening used in Op. 9 #1) 1833

Études in the form of free variations on as theme by Beethoven (Allegretto of Beethoven's Symphony #7; one variation published as Op. 124/2) 1833

6 Concert Studies on Caprices by Paganini (Set II), Op. 10 1833

Sonata #1 in f#, Op. 11 1833-5

Sonata #4 in f (unfinished) 1833-7

Sonata #2 in g, Op. 22 1833-8

Variations sur un nocturne de Chopin (C's Op. 15/3) 1834

Études symphoniques (Symphonic Études), Op. 13 1834; 2nd version 1852

Carnaval, Op. 9 1834-5

Sonata #3 in f, Op. 14, "Concerto without Orchestra" 1835-6; revised 1853

Sonata movement in Bb 1836

Fantasy in C, Op. 17 1836

Davidsbündlertänze, Op. 6 1837

[8] Fantasiestücke, Op. 12 1837

Kinderszenen (Scenes from Childhood), Op. 15 1838

Kreisleriana, Op. 16 1838

[8] Novelletten, Op. 21 1838

4 Clavierstücke, Op. 32 1838-9

Arabesque in C, Op. 18 1839

Blumenstück (Flower Piece) in Db, Op. 19 1839

Humoreske in Bb, Op. 20 1839

[4] Nachtstücke (Night Pieces), Op. 23 1839

Faschingsschwank aus Wien, Op. 26 1839

3 Romances, Op. 28 (bb, F#, B) 1839

Albumblätter (Album leaves), Op. 124 1832-45

4 Fugues, Op. 72 (d, d, f, F) 1845

Album für die Jugend, Op. 68 1848

Waldszenen (Forest Scenes), Op. 82 1848-9

Bunte Blätter (Multicolored Pages), Op. 99 1836-49

4 Marches, Op. 76 (Eb, g, Bb, Eb) 1849

[3] Fantasiestücke, Op. 111 (c, Ab, c) 1851

3 Clavier-sonaten für die Jugend, Op. 118 (G, D, G) 1853

7 Clavierstücke in Fughettenform, Op. 126 1853

Gesänge der Frühe (Songs of the Morning), Op. 133 1853

Theme with Variations in Eb 1854

Canon in Ab, "To Alexis"

Scherzo (rejected from Op. 14) & Presto passionato (original finale of Op. 22)

5 Short Pieces (Notturnino, Ballo, Burla, Capriccio, Écossaise) (nos. 1, 4, & 5 unfinished)

Romanza in f (unfinished)

Piano Duets:

8 Polonaises 1828

Variations on a theme by Prince Louis Ferdinand of Prussia (lost) 1828

Andante & Variations in Bb, Op. 46 (2 pfs; arrmt of chamber version) 1843

Bilder aus Osten (Pictures from the East), Op. 66 1848

12 Pieces, Op. 85 1849

Ball-Scenen (Scenes from a Ball), Op. 109 1851

Kinderball (Children's Ball), Op. 130 1853

Other Keyboard Works:

Studies for the pedal piano, 6 pieces in canon, Op. 56 1845

Studies for the pedal piano, 6 pieces, Op. 58 1845

6 Fugues on B-A-C-H for organ or pedal piano, Op. 60 1845

Piece in F for harmonium (2 mvts) 1849

Stage Works:

Opera, *Der Corsair* (one chorus & one aria only) 1844

Incidental music to Byron's *Manfred*, Op. 115 1848-9

Opera, *Genoveva*, Op. 81 1847-50

Choral Works:

Psalm 150 1822

"Chor von Landleuten," Overture & Chorus 1822

"Tragödie" 1841

"Das Paradies und die Peri," Op. 50 (w/solo voices) 1841-3

Scenes from Goethe's *Faust* (w/ solos) 1844-53

"Adventlied," Op. 71 (w/soprano solo) 1848

"Beim Abschied zu singen," Op. 84 (chorus & winds) 1848

Requiem für Mignon, Op. 98b (w/ solos) 1849

"Nachtlied," Op. 108 1849

"Neujahrslied," Op. 144 1849-50

"Der Rose Pilgerfahrt," Op. 112 (w/ solos) 1851

"Der Königssohn," Op. 116 (w/ solos) 1851

"Des Sängers Fluch," Op. 139 (w/ solos) 1852

"Vom Pagen und der Konigstochter," Op. 140 (w/ solos) 1852

Mass, Op. 147 1852

Requiem, Op. 148 1852

Festival Overture on the "Rheinweinlied," Op. 123 1853

"Das Glück von Edenhall," Op. 143 (w/ solos) 1853

Part Songs:

Der deutsche Rhein
(solo voices, mixed chorus, pf) 1840

6 Lieder, Op. 33
(men's voices)
Der trämende See
Die Minnesänger
Die Lotosblume
Der Zecher als Doctrinair
Rastlose Liebe
Frühlingsglocken 1840

5 Lieder, Op. 55
(mixed voices)
Das Hochlandmädchen
Zahnweh
Mich zieht es nach dem Dörfchen hin
Die gute alte Zeit
Hochlandbursch 1846

4 Gesänge, Op. 59
(mixed voices)
Nord oder Süd
Am Bodensee
Jägerlied
Gute Nacht 1846

3 Gesänge, Op. 62
(men's voices)
Der eidgenossenen Nachtwache
Freiheitslied
Schlachtgesang 1847

Ritornelle in canonischen Weisen, Op. 65
(men's voices)
Die Rose stand im Tau
Laßt Lautenspiel und Becherklang
Blüt' oder Schnee
Gebt mir zu trinken!
Zürne nicht des Herbstes Wind
In Sonnentagen
In Meeres Mitten 1847

3 Partsongs (also Op. 65)
(men's voices)
Zu den Waffen
Schwarz-Rot-Gold
Freiheitssang
(with wind band ad lib) 1848

Romanzen und Balladen, Vol. I, Op. 67
(mixed voices)
Der König in Thule
Schön Rohtraut
Heidenröslein
Ungewitter
John Anderson 1849

Romanzen, Vol. I, Op. 69
(women's voices with pf ad lib)
Tamburinschlägerin
Waldmädchen
Klosterfräulein
Soldatenbraut
Meerfey
Die Capelle 1849

Romanzen und Balladen, Vol. II, Op. 75
(mixed voices)
Schnitter Tod
Im Walde
Der traurige Jäger
Der Rekrut
Vom verwundeten Knaben 1849

Romanzen, Vol. II, Op. 91
(women's voices with pf ad lib)
Rosmarin
Jäger Wohlgemut

Der Wassermann
Das verlassene Mägedelein
Der Bleicherin Nachtlied
In Meeres Mitten 1849

Motet, "Verzweifle nicht im Schmerzenstal," Op. 93
(double chorus with organ ad lib orch'd
  1852 1849

Jagdlieder, Op. 137
(men's voices with 4 horns ad lib)
Zur hohen Jagd
Habet Acht
Jagdmorgen
Frühe
Bei der Flasche 1849

4 doppelchörige Gesänge, Op. 141
(mixed voices)
An die Sterne
Ungewisses Licht
Zuversicht
Talismane 1849

Romanzen und Balladen, Vol. III, Op. 145
(mixed voices)
Der Schmidt
Die Nonne
Der Sänger
John Anderson
Romanze vom Gänsebuben 1849-51

Romanzen und Balladen, Vol. IV, Op.
  146
(mixed voices)
Brautgesang
Bänkelsänger Willie
Der Traum
Sommerlied
Das Schifflein (with flute & horn)
  1849

Am Anfange
(men's voices) n.d.

Vocal Quartets, Trios and Duets with Piano:

3 Gedichte, Op. 29
Ländliches Lied
Lied
Zigeunerleben
(with tambourine and triangle ad lib)
1840

Spanisches Liederspiel, Op. 74
Erste Begegnung (SA)
Intermezzo (TB)
Liebesgram (SA)
In der Nacht (ST)
Es ist verraten (SATB)
Melnacholie (S)
Geständnis (T)
Botschaft (SA)
Ich bin geliebt (SATB)
Appendix: Der Contrabandiste (B)
1849

Minnespiel, Op. 101
Lied (T)
Gesang (S)
Duett (AB)
Lied (T)
Quartett (SATB)
Lied (A)
Duett (ST)
Quartett (SATB) 1849

Spanische Liebeslieder, Op. 138
Vorspiel (pf)
Lied (S)
Lied (T)
Duett (SA)
Romanze (B)
Intermezzo (pf)
Lied (T)
Lied (A)
Duett (TB)
Quartett (SATB) 1849

Die Orange und Myrte (SATB) 1853

3 Lieder für 3 Frauenstimmen, Op. 114
Nänie
Triolett
Spruch

4 Duets, Op. 34
(soprano & tenor)
Liebesgarten
Liebhabers Ständchen
Unter'm Fenster
Familien-Gemälde 1840

3 zweistimmige Lieder, Op. 43
Wenn ich ein Vöglein wär'
Herbstlied
Schön Blümelein 1840

4 Duets, Op. 78
(soprano & tenor)
Tanzlied
Er und sie
Ich denke dein
Wiegenlied 1849

Sommerruh 1849

Mädchenlieder, Op. 103
Mailied
Frülingslied
An die Nachtigall
An den Abendstern 1851

Liedchen von Marie und Papa in F
(unaccompanied) 1852

Lieder:
Verwandlung 1827

Lied für XXX 1827

11 Songs
Sehnsucht (1827)
Die Weinende (1827)
Erinnerung (1828)
Kurzes Erwachen (1828)
Gesanges Erwachen (1828)

Gedichte aus "Liebesfrühling," Op. 37
Der Himmel eine Träne geweint
Er ist gekommen (by Clara
    Schumann)
O ihr Herren
Liebst du um Schönheit (by Clara
    Schumann)
Ich hab' in mich gesogen
Liebste, was kann dies uns scheiden
Schön ist das Fest des Lenzes
Flügel! Flügel! um zu fliegen
Rose, Meer und Sonne
O Sonn! o Meer, o Rose
Warum willst du andre fragen (by Clara
    Schumann)
So wahr die Sonne scheinet 1840

Liederkreis, Op. 39
In der Fremde
Intermezzo
Waldesgespräch
Die Stille
Mondnacht
Schöne Fremde
Auf einer Burg
In der Fremde
Wehmut
Zwielicht
Im Walde
Frühlingsnacht 1840

5 Lieder, Op. 40
Märzveilchen
Muttertraum
Der Soldat
Der Spielmann
Verratene Liebe 1840

Frauenliebe und -leben, Op. 42
Seit ich ihn gesehen
Er. der Herrlichste von allen
Ich kann's nicht fassen
Du Ring an meinem Finger
Helft mir, ihr Schwestern
Süsser Freund, du blickest
An meinem Herzen

Nun hast du mir der ersten Schmerz
    getan 1840

Romanzen und Balladen, Vol. I, Op. 45
Der Schatzgräber
Frühlingsfahrt
Abends am Strand 1840

Dichterliebe, Op. 48
Im wunderschönen Monat Mai
Aus meinen Tränen spriessen
Die Rose, die Lilie
Wenn ich in deine Augen seh'
Ich will meine Seele tauchen
Im Rhein, im heiligen Strome
Ich grolle nicht
Und wüssten's die Blumen
Das ist ein Flöten und Geigen
Hör' ich das Liedchen Klagen
Ein Jüngling liebt ein Mädchen
Am leuchtenden Sommermorgen
Ich hab' im Traum geweinet
Allnächtlich im Traume
Aus alten Märchen winkt es
Die alten, bösen Lieder 1840

Romanzen und Balladen, Vol. II, Op. 49
Die beiden Grenadiere
Die feindlichen Brüder
Die Nonne 1840

Lieder und Gesänge, Vol. II, Op. 51
Sehnsucht
Volksliedchen
Ich wand're nicht
Auf dem Rhein
Liebeslied 1842

Romanzen und Balladen, Vol. III, Op. 53
Blondels Lied
Loreley
Der arme Peter
(a. Die Hands und die Grete;
b. In meiner Brust;
c. Der arme Peter wankt vorbei) 1840

Ballad, "Belsatzar," Op. 57 1840

Romanzen und Balladen, Vol. IV, Op. 64

Die Soldatenbraut

Das verlassene Mägdelein
(a. Entflieh mit mir;
b. Es fiel ein Reif;
c. Auf ihrem Grab [duet])1841-7

Lieder und Gesänge, Vol. III, Op. 77
Der frohe Wandersmann
Mein Garten
Geisternähe
Stiller Vorwurf
Aufträge 1841-50

Der weisse Hirsch (sketches)1848

Liederalbum für die Jugend, Op. 79
Der Abendstern
Schmetterling
Frühlingsbotschaft
Frühlingsgruss
Vom Schlaraffenland
Sonntag
Zigeunerliedchen
Zigeunerliedchen II
Des Knaben Berglied
Mailied (duet ad lib)
Das Käuzlein
Hinaus in's Freie!
Der Sandmann
Marienwürmchen
Die Waise
Das Glück
Weihnachtslied
Die waldelnde Glocke
Frühlingslied
Frühlingsankunft
Die Schwalben
Kinderwacht
Des Sennen Abschied
Er ist's
Spinnelied (trio ad lib)

Des Buben Schützenlied
Schneeglöckchen
Lied Lynceus des Türmers
Mignon 1849

3 Gesänge, Op. 83
Resignation
Die Blume der Ergebung
Der Einsiedler 1850

Ballad, „Der Handschuh," Op. 87 1850

6 Gesänge, Op. 89
Es stürmet am Abendhimmel
Heimliches Verschwinden
Herbstlied
Abschied vom Walde
In's Freie
Röselein, Röselein 1850

6 Gedichte, Op. 90
Lied eines Schmiedes
Meine Rose
Kommen und Scheiden
Die Sennerin
Einsamkeit
Der schwere Abend
Appendix: Requiem 1850

3 Gesänge, Op. 95
Die Tochter Jephthas
An den Mond
Dem Helden 1849

Lieder und Gesänge, Vol. IV, Op. 96
Nachtlied
Schneeglöckchen
Ihre Stimme
Gesungen
Himmel und Erde 1850

Lieder und Gesänge aus "Wilhelm
    Meister," Op. 98a
Kennst du das Land
Ballade des Harfners
Nur wer die Sehnsucht kennt

Wie nie sein Brot mit Tränen aß
Heiss mich nicht reden
Wer sich der Einsamkeit ergibt
Singet nicht in Trauertönen
An die Türen will ich schleichen
So lasst mich scheinen 1849

7 Lieder, Op. 104
Mond, meiner Seele Liebling
Viel Glück zur Reise
Du nennst mich armes Mädchen
Der Zeisig
Reich' mir die Hand
Die letzten Blumen starben
Gekämpft hat meine Barke 1851

6 Gesänge, Op. 107
Herzeleid
Die Fensterscheibe
Der Gärtner
Die Spinnerin
Im Wald
Abendlied 1851-2

4 Husarenlieder, Op. 117
Der Husar, trara!
Der leidige Frieden
Den grünen Zeigern
Da liegt der Feinde gestreckte Schaar 1851

3 Gedichte, Op. 119
Die Hütte
Warnung
Der Bräutigam und die Birke 1851

5 heitere Gesänge, Op. 125
Frühlingslied

Frühlingslust
Die Meerfee
Jung Volkers Lied
Husarenabzug
(alternate sequence 3, 2, 4, 1, 5) 1851

5 Lieder und Gesänge, Op. 127
Sängers Trost
Dein Angesicht
Es leuchter meine Liebe
Mein altes Ross
Schlußlied des Narren 1850-1

Frühlingsgrüße 1851

Gedichte der Königin Maria Stuart, Op. 135
Abschied von Frankreich
Nach der Geburt ihres Sohnes
An die Königin Elisabeth
Abschied von der Welt
Gebet 1852

4 Gesänge, Op. 142
Trost im Gesang
Lehn' deine Wang'
Mädchen-Schwermut
Mein Wagen rollt langsam 1852

Soldatenlied

Die Ammenuhr

Das Schwert

Glocktürmers Töchterlein

Picture Sources

The author and publishers wish to express their thanks to the following sources of illustrative material and/or permission to reproduce it. They will make proper acknowledgements in future editions in the event that any omissions have occurred.

Barbara Meier, Dortmund: pp. 153. Museum of Art and History, Berlin: pp. 22, 60.
National Library -Mendelssohn Collection, Berlin: pp. 44. City Museum, Düsseldorf: pp. 149. Hamburg Art Museum: pp. 116. Heinrich Heine Institute, Düsseldorf: pp. 42. Transport Museum, Dresden: pp. 71. Palatinate Museum, Heidelberg: pp. 20. Lebrecht Music Collection: pp. i, ii, vi, 2, 4, 7, 12, 15, 18, 32, 38, 43, 49, 62, 66, 67, 70, 76, 80, 85, 110, 139, 140, 144, 146. City Art Museum, Liepzig: pp. 10, 101. Robert Schumann House, Zwickau: pp. 3, 6, 11, 16, 34, 39, 41, 52, 80, 99, 102, 120, 123, 127, 129, 142, 151. Rowohlt Archive, Hamburg: pp. 50, 91.

Index

Shakespeare, William, 66, 83
Sohn, Carl, 133
Sontag, Henriette, 115
Sörgel (viola player), 14
Spanish, 19
Speyer, 19
Spohr, Louis, 41, 83, 84, 98, 131; Violin
    Concerto, Op 47, 89
Sterndale Bennett, William, 37, 43, 46,
    56, 82
Stifter, Adalbert, 115
Stravinsky, Igor, 51

Täglichsbeck (violin player), 14
Tausch, Julius, 134, 138–9, 147
Thalberg, Sigismund, 69, 81, 82, 84
The Hague, 89
Thibaut, Justus, 18–20, 23
Tieck, Ludwig, 38, 118, 120
Tver, 104

Verhulst, Johannes, 72, 82, 107
Viardot, Pauline, 82, 104, 115
Vienna, 24, 61, 65, 68–70, 114, 115,
    147, 150; censorship in, 69–70;
    Conservatory, 117; *Ludlamshöhle*, 39;
    uprising, 128
Vieuxtemps, Henri, 56
virtuosi, 32, 45, 62
Voigt, Carl, 93, 97
Voigt, Henriette, 30, 56–7

Wagner, Richard, 83, 125, 133; in
    Dresden, 108; Schumann's opinion
    of, 109; flees Dresden, 117, 129;
    Schumann's relations with, 122; Liszt
    aligned with, 130; *Lohengrin*, 109,
    119, 122; Symphony in C major,
    33–4, 109; *Tannhäuser*, 109, 119

Walther (friend), 8
Wasielewski, Joseph Wilhelm von, 101,
    133–4, 136, 149–50
Weber, Carl Maria von, 4, 28, 39, 98,
    118, 126; *Invitation to the Dance*, 30
Weber, Gottfried, 41
Weichsel, River, 104
Weimar, 28, 89, 92, 138
Wieck, Alwin, 15, 27, 28
Wieck, Clara, *see* Schumann, Clara (née
    Wieck)
Wieck, Friedrich, 15, 23, 31; as
    Schumann's teacher, 16–17, 27–8;
    character, 28; as member of League
    of David, 39; founder of Schumann's
    journal, 41; and Clara's career, 49,
    61, 70–1; animosity towards
    Schumann, 52, 59, 61, 68, 93; legal
    case against Schumann, 71–3; takes
    up Clara's rival, 81; reconciliation
    with Robert and Clara, 101–2; con-
    tinuing tension with Schumann, 108
Wieck, Gustav, 15, 27
Wieck, Marianne (née Tromlitz, later
    Bargiel), 15, 27, 149
Wieck, Marie, 108, 111
Wiedebein, Gottlob, 15, 17
Wielhorski, Count, 104
Wigand (publisher), 150
Wittgenstein, Princess, 133
Worms, 19

Zelter, Carl Friedrich, 5
Zuccalmaglio, Anton Wilhelm von, 39,
    82
Zwickau, 2, 4–5, 9, 19, 33, 52, 89;
    'Bürge Konsert', 5–6; Lyceum, 2, 5,
    10; Marienkirche, 6; Music Society,
    21; Schumann festival, 99, 117